THE ART
OF
HOMEMAKING

THE ART

OF

HOMEMAKING

by
DARYL V. HOOLE

Illustrated by Dick & Mary Scopes

Published by
Deseret Book Company
Salt Lake City, Utah
1969

3rd Edition, Revised and Enlarged

16th Printing, 1976

LITHOGRAPHED IN U.S.A. BY

PUBLISHERS PRESS
SALT LAKE CITY, UTAH

To my daughters, Jean, Diane,
Elaine, Becky and Nancy, who
I hope will grow up to be
happy homemakers.

INTRODUCTION

It is intended that women be happy and successful in their homemaking. Being a homemaker is a divine appointment and is a woman's greatest calling. It should be rich in the rewards of joy, satisfaction and accomplishment.

All too often, however, women feel confused, distraught or bored with their role as homemakers. They frequently dread each day, live for the time when their children will be raised so they can be released from it all, or they escape from their responsibilities to their home and family and return to the business world.

Other women do enjoy their homemaking activities but find their work consumes most of their day and there is little time for other interests.

Many women are wonderful homemakers and managers but are eager for new ideas and skills to make their homemaking even more effective and satisfying.

To all of these women, this book offers a practical guide to happier homemaking. It recalls to mind the significance of homemaking and gives their attitude a lift. When the suggestions concerning order and efficiency, methods and approaches are applied, coupled with the workable plan which systematizes the routine duties, women will find their interest in homemaking greatly increasing and that there will be time to get their work done and enjoy creative activities, family fun and personal development.

This is not just a book on how to keep house; it offers a way of life which will bring joy and satisfaction to the homemaker and rich, happy experiences to every family member.

ACKNOWLEDGMENTS

The preparation of this material has been made possible because of the ideal example and teachings of my mother, Mrs. Donovan H. Van Dam, because of Mrs. Alan H. Parsons, Mrs. Douglas Williams, Mrs. Vesta Barnett, Mrs. Eileen Gibbons Kump, Mrs. Douglas D. Alder and because of the cooperation and consideration of my wonderful husband.

CONTENTS

THE IDEAL HOMEMAKER

Grandmother, on a winter's day, milked the cows and fed them hay, slopped the hogs, saddled the mule, then got the children off to school, did a washing, mopped the floors, washed the windows, and did some chores; cooked a dish of home-dried fruit, pressed her husband's Sunday suit.

Swept the parlor, made the bed, baked a dozen loaves of bread, split some firewood, and then lugged in enough to fill the kitchen bin; cleaned the lamps and put in oil, stewed some apples she thought would spoil; churned the butter, baked a cake, then exclaimed, "For heaven's sake, the calves have got out of the pen!"—went out and chased them in again.

Gathered the eggs and locked the stable, back to the house and set the table, cooked a supper that was delicious, and afterward washed up all the dishes, fed the cat and sprinkled the clothes, mended a basketful of hose; then opened the organ and began to play, "When You Come to the End of a Perfect Day."

Author Unknown

This grandmother knew the art of homemaking! Although today the demands and activities of a homemaker have changed somewhat, the abilities and attitudes required have remained the same. We modern homemakers want to be like this grandmother, able to perform each day the tasks required of us and feel happy about doing so.

Of course it is normal for every homemaker to have bad days when little is accomplished and when she doesn't feel like it has been a perfect day at all. In fact, at times she might be completely discouraged and depressed with her role in life. It is the purpose of this book to help you with those bad days and feelings of exasperation so that they will become infrequent and fleeting.

Let's begin by defining an ideal homemaker. An ideal is something for which we strive. It is our standard of perfection and excellence. An ideal, or a goal, is like the North Star which guides the mariners at sea. Although they never reach the North Star, it keeps them charting their course in the right direction. We can't be ideal homemakers in every way at all times, but we do need a goal to be our North Star and to help us along in the right direction.

For my goal, I like to think of an ideal homemaker as a diamond, perfectly cut so as to bring out countless beautiful highlights. Just as each diamond is cut a little differently in order to make many facets, so is each homemaker a distinct individual with her own special traits and talents. But in both diamonds and homemakers, certain qualities must be present if each is to sparkle brilliantly and thereby be valued and cherished.

FACET NO. 1 An ideal homemaker is lovely to look at and lovely to be around—she has a wholesome attitude and a pleasing appearance. She has the courage to be happy and strives to live above the grievous faults of moodiness, sulkiness, and complaining. She is gracious and thoughtful and is consequently adored by her family and admired by all who know her. This facet means true beauty in her diamond.

FACET NO. 2 An ideal homemaker is ambitious and enthusiastic through application of the law that how one feels emotionally greatly determines how she feels physically. She finds that a creative approach to homemaking gives her the "pep pill" she needs and causes her to be an especially sparkling diamond.

FACET NO. 3 An ideal homemaker is devoted to the great career in which she is engaged. She is a professional in her field by being a homemaker every day and letting her devotion and sense of duty, rather than her moods, dominate her. This makes her truly genuine as a diamond.

FACET NO. 4 An ideal homemaker realizes that order must be the first law of her home. With her home free from clutter and confusion, maximum progress and accomplishment may be enjoyed by family members. This helps bring about a tranquil atmosphere which is a blessing to all. Such a facet in her diamond makes it truly a brilliant one.

FACET NO. 5 An ideal homemaker makes the best use of her time and energy by being efficient so that she is able to not only keep up with her housework, but she is able to be a companion to her husband and a friend and teacher to her children. She is also able to pursue some personal interests which contribute to her happiness and development. Having such a facet in her diamond does much to enhance her worth.

FACET NO. 6 An ideal homemaker realizes that many of life's choicest blessings are gained through hard work, and she therefore accepts work as a challenge and an opportunity rather than a burden. This facet gives her real quality as a diamond.

FACET NO. 7 An ideal homemaker plans a program or a schedule for each day so that she is the master, rather than the victim, of her work. This facet lends true value to her as a diamond.

FACET NO. 8 An ideal homemaker is prepared to perpetuate the good things she learned in her own home and is ever alert to new ideas and hints which will make her work more effective and help her to be an increasingly better homemaker. This way her diamond becomes more beautiful over the years.

FACET NO. 9 An ideal homemaker is consistent in applying the best skills and methods she knows. She has a built-in self-starter. This makes her rare indeed.

FACET NO. 10 An ideal homemaker's activities are well balanced. Though she may be noted for a specialty and devote a major part of her time to one particular phase, she doesn't spend all of her time cooking, nor does she concentrate just on sewing, or on cleaning, or on reading, or on outside interests. She reaches out to include in her life stimulating projects which serve as an incentive to her. This gives her diamond a beautiful cut.

FACET NO. 11 An ideal homemaker is able to transform four walls into a home by creating both spiritual and physical beauty therein. A true diamond enhances everything it touches.

FACET No. 12 She will be ideal in her role as a homemaker,

not only because of the countless current values, but because her example and teachings will live at least another generation through her children. She must help them to be valuable diamonds too.

FACET NO. 13 An ideal homemaker will encourage family traditions to add color and depth to the great picture she is painting. Instead of her home being just a "short-order house," it will be a hallowed place where children learn life's great lessons, gain proper values, and build memories which will enrich their lives and help determine their destinies. She knows that to be a mother in the highest sense of the word will add the facet of eternal worth to her diamond.

FACET No. 14 An ideal homemaker exercises patience, under-standing, and imperturbability unless controlled anger and reason-able discipline are justified. She will do her best to take those occasional "bad days," when everything seems to go wrong, in her stride, realizing that she needs some valleys in order to appreciate the mountains. She needs a sense of humor. She should not take herself, her house, or her children *too* seriously. Then like a real diamond, which is the hardest naturally occurring substance known, she is able to withstand life's blows.

FACET NO. 15 An ideal homemaker is the type of companion and wife who merits the appreciation and cooperation of her husband and helps him to want to do his part well as a husband, father, and provider. Only then is she of true value.

FACET NO. 16 An ideal homemaker is skilled in the handling of money, in intelligent shopping, in careful storage, and in clever preparation of food. She is able to conserve the family's possessions through good management. She doesn't economize out of self-pity, but because it is a challenge to get the very most out of the resources available. Just as with diamonds, skill and talent are used to make the most of what is available.

FACET NO. 17 And after all of these facets have made our ideal homemaker like a sparkling diamond, she will add a few other special facets of her own to set her apart from all the rest.

FACET NO. 18 An ideal homemaker is an artist in general management so that her home is able to function at its peak performance and fulfill its lofty purpose, and so that she, along with her husband and children, can reflect the joy, order and progressive spirit therein. She doesn't try to accomplish this thirty years at a time, but strives to practice being an artist in management and homemaking JUST FOR TODAY. This makes her a diamond of radiant colors and highlights.

FACET NO. 19 An ideal homemaker will seek divine guidance through prayer, so that her home may be an extension of heaven, and so that she may walk in partnership with God in rearing the precious little souls he has sent her. This will add the facet of purity to her diamond.

FACET NO. 20 An ideal homemaker, through having these many facets in her brilliant diamond, will be able to take pride in her noble calling and in the great work she is doing.

(One woman, after reading this list of facets, decided the best thing she could do for her family was put her children up for adoption! Seriously, check over the list of facets carefully. You'll probably be amazed at how many of them you have already mastered. Then let this book help you make the remaining ones part of your homemaking prowess.)

It is sad to hear a woman lament, "I'm just a housewife." If only she could realize that she is a homemaker by divine appointment. Making a home is a special mission for a woman. It is no accident. This is where God intended her to be. This is the task for which she was created. This task is second in importance to none.

Some women have felt the career as a homemaker an insult to their intelligence and abilities. Actually, running a home challenges any other role in requiring intelligence, ingenuity, and abilities unnumbered. It can offer the most noble accomplishment and can bring the greatest joy and satisfaction of any type of work. We women must be proud to be homemakers.

The lovelier you are, the more educated you are—either formally or otherwise, the more talented and capable and accomplished you are, the richer can be your life and that of your family if you're truly a homemaker, not just a housewife.

We are especially fortunate to be homemakers in this century when modern equipment and automation have removed much of the so-called drudgery from housework. It is a blessing to live in a land where fine appliances such as automatic washing machines are in abundance, where newly developed chemical solutions such as cleaning aids are available, and where time-saving materials such as permanent-press clothes and plastics are plentiful.

Years ago when our grandmothers prepared to do the family wash, they first had to spend hours making their own soap. Then they would have to haul water by buckets from the well, chop wood for a fire, and then labor hard and long to clean the clothes with the aid of the harsh soap and a scrubbing board. Our grandmothers' washday was a long exhausting one.

Just think, all that many of us have to do is turn a knob and push a button!

Each generation has its own challenge, however, Even though much of the physical labor has been done away with, we have other difficult problems. We live in a very complex, fast age. Much is required of us. We no longer just clean, cook and sew. Today we're expected to be dieticians, home executives, psychologists and the family purchasing agent. There are lots of pressures and the emotional strain is very taxing. How can we cope with all this? How can we keep up with the demands and still enjoy some of the old-fashioned happiness, serenity and peace of mind which made family living so worthwhile a generation ago? This is why women today are eager to learn about home management.

With an understanding of the importance and significance of homemaking and with an appreciation for the modern aids we

have, the next step is to realize the purpose behind our work.

Sir Christopher Wren, the famous English architect and designer of St. Paul's Cathedral, visited the spot where the cathedral was being constructed. He approached a workman and asked him what he was doing. "I'm cutting stone," the man replied.

He inquired of a second construction worker. This man replied, "I'm building a building for Christopher Wren."

Then the architect asked a third worker. He answered, "I'm building a cathedral to God."

You know, you can be mighty tired and discouraged by evening if you have done nothing but the same old thing all day long: clean up messes, move dirt from one place to another, change and wash diapers, do the same dishes you washed yesterday.

On the other hand, if you spend the day making your house a lovely home and caring for precious little children, at nightfall you feel as though you've had a touch of heaven in your home, and you have a sense of joy and accomplishment. Like the workman who was building a cathedral to God, you are able to visualize the over-all purpose of your work. Being a homemaker has real meaning for you.

Each of us is richly blessed to be engaged in this greatest of all careers as indicated in this verse:

> God, give each true, good woman
>   Her own, small house to keep—
> No heart should ache with longing—
>   No hurt should go too deep—
> Guard her age-old desire—
>   A house to love and sweep.
> Give her a man beside her.
>   A kind man—and a true—

And let them work together
   And love—a lifetime through.
And let her mother children
   As gentle women do.
Give her a shelf for dishes,
   And a shining box for bread,
A white cloth for her table,
   And a white spread for her bed.
A shaded lamp at nightfall,
   And a row of books much read.

God, let her work with laughter,
   And let her rest with sleep;
No life can truly offer
   A peace more sure and deep—
God, give each true good woman
   Her own small house to keep.

Grace Noel Crowell

FACET NO. 1
THE TWO "A's"

An ideal homemaker is lovely to look at and lovely to be around—she has a wholesome attitude and a pleasing appearance. She has the courage to be happy and strives to live above the faults of moodiness, sulkiness, and complaining. She is gracious and thoughtful and is consequently adored by her family and admired by all who know her.

ATTITUDE

A lady who was annoyed by the incessant piano practicing of someone in a neighboring hotel suite called the manager and insisted that the man limit his practicing hours.

The hotel manager replied, "Lady, I don't believe you understand. The man is Paderewski, and he is practicing for his next great concert."

The lady immediately called her friends and invited them to her suite so that they, too, could enjoy the beautiful music with her.

Her attitude made the difference!

William James, the great Harvard psychologist, said: "The greatest discovery of my generation is that you can change your circumstances by changing your attitudes of mind."

Here are three typical attitudes toward housework. As you read them, you may identify yourself with one of them.

1. "Work is a duty so important that its accomplishment must be given priority over whatever else needs attention."

Women who feel this way forget that work is a means to an end and they regard it as the end itself. Actually, the happy family is the desired end result; work should be just the stepping stones leading to this. Sometimes we get it all backwards like this: a man was scheduled for surgery in a hospital one day, but his wife was unable to accompany him because it was Monday and she always washed on Monday!

2. "Work is a necessary evil so I'll get it over as quickly as possible."

There are many women who feel this way. They don't enjoy their work; in fact, they resent it and begrudge the time it takes. This is a negative attitude which certainly shows in their lives and is reflected in the lives of their family members.

Let's look at housework objectively, instead. I do believe in getting it done quickly and well, but not because it is a necessary evil. To me, the routine housework is a foundation, and the quicker and better I can lay the foundation each morning, the higher I can build during the day.

Some women spend the entire morning trying to lay the foundation. It seems it takes them forever to get the beds made, the table cleared and the crumbs swept up. There is little time left for them to build.

Other women try to build before they lay the foundation. Before the beds are made and the table is cleared and the dishes are done, they will start on a project, such as scrubbing and waxing a floor, cleaning out a closet, washing the windows, making a dress, or reading a book.

Later in the day should anyone drop in, the visitor fails to see the shiny floors, sparkling windows or the newly made dress, but instead her gaze meets the unmade beds and the dirty, cluttered kitchen. The homemaker is embarrassed to tears.

No matter how clean your house might be, it won't show it if beds are unmade and things are cluttered. Even though there may be a little dust lurking somewhere, your house will still look all right if it is in order.

Don't work backwards. Without a foundation things will crumble!

3. "Work is a creative experience. Not every job is equally creative, but most are stimulating and rewarding. I will do my best to

make every piece of work I do a challenge and a pleasant experience by thinking of the results rather than the process."

Quotations by
Rhea Gardner

Of course, the third attitude toward housework is the ideal one. The homemaker who will be happy will determine to condition her attitude so as to make her work a satisfying, creative experience. This way her home will truly be "Home, sweet home."

At the grocery store one day I heard this comment about a neighbor: "She's a screaming maniac. It's no wonder her husband is always busy with his business or doing church work. The neighborhood children seldom go there to play. In fact, they even cross the street to avoid passing her home." This is a sad situation. Something has gone wrong—her poor attitude is at the bottom of it all. She was such a lovely girl years ago when her husband courted her and fell in love with her.

So, Mrs. Homemaker, remain the sweet person you were as a bride!

Once in a while take out your wedding picture and look at it honestly. How do you compare today? You may have accumulated some gray hairs or wrinkles since you said, "I do," but husbands don't mind that. Make certain that sweetness is still there. Is it? That's what counts!

It could help your attitude a great deal to frequently recall to mind stories like this one as told by a young mother:

"It had been one of my usual busy days—housework, cleaning and caring for the children—jobs that I would repeat the next day and the next. But it had been an exciting day for my five-year-old son. A group of youngsters from our church had been taken to visit some shut-ins. Johnny came

home bubbling with talk of the trip and the sick ladies. I put Johnny to bed a little earlier that evening, and as is our bedtime custom, I listened as he said his prayers. This night his prayer was different. 'And please, God,' he added, 'please help those ladies get well so they can hang out clothes and wash dishes like Mommie.' I stood there in the darkened room, looking down at Johnny's sleepy head on the pillow. It was a moment of quiet revelation. I felt humble—the very best that my son could hope for someone else was a life just like mine. Suddenly the morning's dirty dishes and unmade beds became my blessings."

Perhaps a poem like this one over your kitchen sink might be just the thought you (or your children) need to tackle another batch of dishes.

> Thank God for dirty dishes,
> They have a tale to tell;
> While other folks go hungry,
> We're eating very well.
>
> With home and health and happiness
> We shouldn't want to fuss,
> For by this stack of evidence,
> God's very good to us.
>
> "Dear Abby" column

Someone wisely stated: "Attitude begins with Gratitude." The first step towards improving your attitude would be:

Gain an appreciation of your calling as a homemaker.

Second, learn to visualize the over-all purpose of your work.

Third, be at your physical best at all times—both in appearance and health. (If you don't feel well, see a doctor!)

Fourth, take steps to secure good relationships between you and your husband and you and your children.

Fifth, learn and practice good homemaking skills. (Skills bring thrills!)

Sixth, analyze yourself and be willing to overcome personal problems.

Seventh, plan frequent association with people who have good attitudes.

Eighth, keep busy so you'll have only enough time to *think positively.* COUNT YOUR BLESSINGS!

>Promise yourself success
>At the beginning of each day.
>And you'll be surprised how often
>Things turn out that way.
>
>Dr. Norman Vincent Peale

APPEARANCE

Not only is your attitude of great importance, but your appearance also plays a vital role in a happy home. One of the most common complaints unhappy husbands have is that their wives have neglected their appearance and slop around the house with uncombed hair and in runover slippers which look like two dead rabbits. If for no other reason than to keep the romance alive in your marriage, it is worth it to put your best self forward. Each morning get up and get completely dressed.

This should happen the very first thing! If you don't dress promptly, pretty soon its 8:00, 9:00, 9:30 and the morning goes. Until you're dressed you're not prepared for anything. Once you are dressed, everything works out better. The sooner you're dressed, the more successful is your day.

Getting dressed means putting on something that is comfortable, combing your hair, applying some make-up, and putting on shoes. Shoes which support you well will do wonders to eliminate fatigue and leg and backaches. If you wear shoes which are too flat or too flimsy, you'll be tired all day. Don't be just two feet from happiness!

Dressing takes such a few minutes, and besides making your husband happy, you'll find that you feel much more eager and ready to begin your day's work. You'll find that your work goes much faster and smoother if you are properly dressed for it than if you're impeded by a flapping housecoat and slipping scuffies. If you LOOK THE PART, you'll feel like DOING THE PART. And, remember, as far as make-up is concerned, "Even a barn looks better if it's painted!"

A sign in a beauty shop reads:

BEAUTY IS A DUTY

After attending a homemaking class where this was discussed, one lady's husband asked her what she had learned. She replied, "I learned to get dressed first thing each morning."

"Great," he exclaimed, "we already have our money's worth!"

Another lady reported that it didn't help at all at her house. The morning following the class she did get up and get dressed promptly, but her little toddler spent the entire morning clinging to her skirt. He thought she was leaving him! She went on to say that it was several mornings later before he understood that Mother was not going away but that she had just turned over a new leaf! The real pay-off came when she over-heard her teenage daughter telling her friends of the improvements and changes which were taking place in their home lately. Then the daughter added, "And Mother is even dressed for breakfast!"

Mrs. Homemaker, you owe it to your husband and children to get dressed promptly each morning. More important, you owe it to yourself. People place whatever value on you which you place on yourself. If you look like the family doormat they'll walk all over you. If you look pert, neat and attractive and as though you had some opinions and rights, they will respect you for it and cooperate better. As you lay the foundation of routine work for a successful day, getting dressed is the corner stone.

Your appearance can help you in more than just a psychological way. In a purely physical way, attention given to your appearance can be important to your vitality and effectiveness. I am talking about posture. Every part of your body functions better if you stand, walk, and sit correctly, and your energy depends to a great extent on the amount of oxygen in your blood. Slumping shoulders cramp one's lungs, a curving back is conducive to backaches, foot pains, or even indigestion.

John B. Kress, civilian supervisor of calisthenics at West Point, says, "Posture is not a static position. It's the way we stand and walk and sit and bend and reach." The three body points to watch are the positions of the shoulders, the pelvis, and the feet; shoulders: back and down; pelvis: tipped up in front, held down in back; feet: toes pointed straight ahead. When any of these three body parts is positioned incorrectly, the whole body is distorted in compensation for the one mistake. Once we realize this, it becomes worth the effort to strive for a better posture. A few minutes of exercise each day, to strengthen weak spots, or else a few minutes of an exaggerated "West Point Stance," may be all that is necessary.

Some people sigh at the very thought of exercise. Actually, it is a wonderful aid in reducing tension and nervousness. Anyone who has taught the junior groups in Sunday School will remember how a rest exercise relaxes the children so they can enjoy the remainder of the lesson.

Evelyn Loewendahl, physical education expert, says, "When you are tired or tense, the best pick-me-up is a few minutes of exercise." And contrary to some opinion, you do not need leotards and a tumbling mat to exercise. Two exercises which can be done while watching television or waiting for the water to run in the bathtub are these: clasp your hands together behind your back, roll your shoulders back as far as possible, pull down tightly with arms. Hold——relax. Repeat five or more times. And: standing with arms straight overhead, feet apart, bend *loosely* and let arms swing between legs. Swing back up to first position. Stretch——relax. Repeat five or ten times.

If even these very simple exercises sound too much for you, then simply run in place or stand with the most perfect posture you are able to affect and take five deep breaths several times a day. This will help you look and feel better and work better!

FACET NO. 2
ANOTHER "A"

An ideal homemaker is ambitious and enthusi-
astic through application of the law that how
one feels emotionally greatly determines how
she feels physically.

Someone once said, "Persistence-Energy-Power" and coined the word "PEP."

Everyone has occasions when he is exhausted, and justifiably so, but some people are always tired—they even wake up tired. If a physical examination proves all is well, perhaps a mental check-up would be in order.

One evening a housewife was so tired that she decided to let the dinner dishes go until the next morning. A little later friends called and invited her and her husband to go square dancing that evening. She responded eagerly to the invitation and had a delightful time whirling around the floor. She wasn't tired of activity; she was just tired of doing the dishes. She needed a change. She needed some interesting activity to look forward to and to help her get through the dishes.

It takes a mighty discerning person to tell the difference between tiredness and laziness!

It is interesting to note as you observe ambitious people that the more one does, the more he is able to do because ENERGY GROWS WITH USE. William James said, "Excitements, ideas, and efforts are what give energy."

Boredom, like fatigue, creeps in when our imagination breaks down. We are bored when our ideas are exhausted, when we can find no new frontiers to explore, when we have lost interest in our work.

There are women who feel bored even when they have several small children to care for, dishes piled in the sink, clothes to wash, and a dirty house to clean. They aren't bored because of a lack of things to do, but rather due to a lack of stimulus. They regard their housework as futile because they are not able to manage it properly and because they do not understand its over-all purpose and are not able to visualize the rewards. Their boredom has developed into a chronic case of inertia, and there they sit—the housework mounting right along with their contempt for it as well as for themselves. These women need special help with the attitudes and skills of homemaking.

Some other women are bored because they feel there really is not enough in the home to keep them busy. Perhaps their families are small or their children are grown, and after several hours of routine work each morning they have nothing but a l-o-n-g day to look forward to. The antidote to such a situation is a shot of imagination. Such things as reading, sewing, decorating, music, outdoor life, interest in people and a desire to be of service to them are excellent cures for the malady of boredom. (See Facet No. 10, INCENTIVE PLAN, for details regarding this.) One word of caution, however: time-killers, such as too much or the wrong type of television shows and movies or sensational stories, offer only a momentary illusion of having a purpose in life and afterwards one's boredom and restlessness is more intense than ever. Seek activities which, instead of being busy work and escapes, are purposeful and edifying.

So, remember THE TWO "A's" and THE OTHER "A":

Keep your Attitude right by thinking of the results, rather than the process of your housework.

Be Attractive and well-groomed at all times.

By feeling right on the inside and looking fine on the

outside and by being interested in your work and keeping your imagination and ideas alive, you'll find you have "PEP" and Ambition.

FACET NO. 3
SOME ARE ALMOSTERS

An ideal homemaker is devoted to the great career in which she is engaged. She is a professional in her field by being a homemaker every day and letting her devotion and sense of duty, rather than her moods, dominate her.

If we were to divide all of the homemakers we know into general types, we would likely come to this conclusion:

There are three types. The first category consists of the *"Don't Cares."* These women are content to exist in a mess of confusion, dust, and fingerprints. The result of their complacency is more mess, more dust, and more fingerprints.

Then there are the *"Almosters."* They just don't quite make it, like the car brakes that almost worked, or the man who almost caught the train. Their intentions are good, and they almost make it. They spend lots of time and energy, but they don't quite reach their goals, they don't quite get the job done. Their houses are never quite clean, their ironing is never quite caught up, they are never quite ready, or quite on time. This results in frustrations, wear and tear on the nerves, damage to self-respect, and failure to meet important goals and opportunities.

There is lots of hope for the Almosters, however. Most of them are putting forth the time and energy. All they need is some direction to their activities and they can be good managers and ideal homemakers.

Fortunately, there are many *Ideal Homemakers* among women. They are the ones who are able to keep up with the countless demands of homemaking and make their homes

function smoothly. The results of their abilities are joy and satisfaction, peace of mind, and a rich interesting life.

You are not a "Don't Care"—your very interest in this book indicates that you DO CARE about the wonderful work of being a worthy wife and mother. You are determined to succeed in this great role.

You will never have to submit a letter to a newspaper counselor, resulting in a caption such as this one which appeared in the Mary Marker column of the *Deseret News*.

" 'I'm a Total Failure in Life," Laments Mother"

Instead you might write a letter such as the one which appeared a few days later in the same column and was captioned:

"Happy Homemaker Tells Work Schedule"

This second woman told how she had overcome some very similar difficulties in her life through a deep desire to improve and the determination to do so. Through her efforts she is now a happy, successful homemaker.

A newspaper article recently reported that under certain circumstances, people have super-human strength. A mother, seeing that her son was pinned under an automobile which he had been repairing and who was in danger of being crushed to death, lifted the 3,500-pound car off the boy. After the incident she tried to lift the car again for the benefit of newspaper reporters and photographers, but she was unable to do so because this time she didn't HAVE TO. The article pointed out that a person can do anything if he really wants to. It confirmed the old adage: "Where there is a will, there is a way."

Vaslav Nijensky, one of the great ballet stars of all time, was known for his five-feet leaps. But not only could he leap higher than any other dancer, he could hover a second or so at the mid-point of his leaps. Now anyone knows that it is impossible for a human being to hover in mid-air, but Vaslav Nijensky was doing it. His audiences always asked him HOW. "It's easy," he responded. "I just made up my mind to do it."

"Just made up my mind. . . ." To want to, to have to . . . These are vital steps toward changing your ways or getting a job done. But they aren't the whole story. There is something else of even greater importance.

As necessary as determination and will power are, when they come into conflict with one's self-image,* the self-image invariably wins. In order to master these homemaking skills and ideas, it might be necessary for you to first build your self-image. This self-image is a clear mental picture of how you see yourself to be. Everything you do is consistent with your self-image. In order to change your ways, you must change your self-image. You become what you think, so think of yourself the way you want to be.

Let your imagination carry you through a desired situation in your home or with your family—imagine every minute detail. Make it a happy, successful situation. Let your mind's eye see everything you do—in the right way—and let your mind's ear hear everything you say which, too, will be just the right thing to say. Indulge in some generous daydreaming. See yourself as you want to be.

Can you visualize yourself just as your husband is coming home for dinner? You greet him at the door with a smile and a kiss. You look pert, attractive and well-groomed. The kitchen presents a well-set table, and the aroma of a delicious dinner is tantalizing to the appetite. The children are happy and are playing or studying contentedly. The house is orderly and is sparkling clean. You feel at peace with yourself because today's

*For more information on self-image see Maxwell Maltz, *Psycho Cybernetics* (Englewood Cliffs, N. J.: Prentice-Hall, Inc., 1960).

work has been done today. The stage is set for an ideal dinner hour and a pleasant evening to follow.

Let your thoughts soar and see yourself as a very efficient type of person who gets the job done. Imagine everything you would do or say.

Let your imagination give you the thrill of planning your work and then working your plan. Dream of the excitement you would feel as you see your plans materialize.

Imagine yourself as a patient, understanding, wonderful mother whose children feel very close to you and who are responding well to your love and influence. In your mind, practice everything such a mother would do and say.

Imagine yourself as a happy, successful homemaker. Let your creative imagination give you some ideal experiences—if you haven't had enough actual ones—and you'll become a happy, effective homemaker.

No one wants to be just an "Almoster." Let's continue our analysis (discussion) by suggesting the qualities and characteristics which make an ideal homemaker.

FACET NO. 4

A PLACE FOR EVERYTHING—
EVERYTHING IN ITS PLACE

An ideal homemaker realizes that order must be the first law of her home. With her home free from clutter and confusion, maximum progress and accomplishment may be enjoyed by family members. This helps bring about a tranquil atmosphere which is a blessing to all.

The story is told of a giant who visited the land of the pigmies. He roared with laughter at the tiny bodies and the great pretensions of those miniature folk. He ridiculed their weakness and insignificance, but when he fell asleep, they bound him with innumerable threads and he awoke to find himself a helpless captive.

The pigmies and the threads they used were just little things compared to the size of the giant, but all together their strength was greater than his. SUCH IS THE POWER OF HABIT—small, weak, and insignificant in its beginning, but strong as a band of iron when frequently repeated to become part of our character.

Habits can make or break us as homemakers. Habits become so automatic that we never even think about them or notice them, but oh, their effects. . . .

ORDER IS ONE OF THE FIRST LAWS OF HEAVEN. It is essential in the heavens; otherwise chaos would rule. Order is just as essential in our homes, if, instead of chaos, we want a neat, smoothly functioning home and peace of mind. It can become every bit as easy to put clothes, papers, books, and other items WHERE THEY BELONG as to throw them over a chair, on a table or on the mantle. It is all a matter of habit.

A young mother of five children lamented: "I cleaned house the entire day yesterday, and then today we all got ready for a picnic and just threw clothes and picnic supplies. Each room is as littered as if there had been a New Year's Eve Party. No one would ever know I had cleaned. Just think, all of that time and energy has gone to waste."

In just a few more minutes' time, each older child could have helped put away the clothes and straightened up the kitchen, and then each room could have been left neat and orderly. Mother's work from the previous day wouldn't have been in vain. It is merely a matter of THOUGHT, TRAINING, and HABIT.

It is significant to note that even before this person was married and had children, she was careless and untidy with regard to her belongings. ORDERLINESS IS BASIC WITH AN INDIVIDUAL and has little to do with the number of children in the family, except for the fact that when the children are young, toys will be scattered on the floor while youngsters are playing. That is understandable.

The clutter with which we're concerned is the newspapers strewn around, the shoes and articles of clothing which should have been put away, the unanswered mail scattered about, the apple cores and scraps of paper which should be discarded, and on and on. We as homemakers, set the standards for the orderliness in our homes. It is basic with us. Children are only an excuse, not a reason, for a cluttered house. I have seen mothers with families of seven, eight or nine children managing beautifully. Sometimes young college girls in dormitories live in such a slothful way. It's up to you! Once your example is established, you'll be ready for the next step: that of helping your husband and children to keep order. This will be treated in subsequent chapters. But for right now, let's go back to your part.

Some people justify their untidiness by claiming that it takes too much time to be neat; they would rather do something "creative" with their time. Perhaps it does require a second's more time to be neat and orderly initially, but ultimately considerable time is saved by not having to hunt for a pencil, the mate to a shoe, or the other stocking.

Housecleaning can be done much more smoothly and faster if things are where they belong and you don't have to shift and restack as you work. It takes longer to set something down, to be picked up later and put away, than it does to put it away in the first place. ORDER would come out way ahead in a race with CONFUSION.

A mother of seven young children confessed that after nineteen years of careless housekeeping she finally gained the desire and determination to have a well-ordered house. She said: "The result was just like magic. When I began to function as a homemaker, my husband took renewed interest in his work and became a better provider; my children were more cooperative and became better students at school; and with the nerve-wracking confusion removed, everyone's disposition improved. Some very serious problems have been solved since I decided to make our house a home." So the importance of order in the home is more than just for appearance sake. Order helps a home to run smoothly and well, much frustration and time are saved because anything can be located, order sets the stage for power and accomplishment, and when a home reflects tender loving care, everyone benefits.

Now, how to establish and maintain order:

First: LET EACH ROOM FULFILL ITS FUNCTION.

I believe that except for very unusual occasions, the bedrooms should be used for sleeping, the kitchen for eating, and the living room for relaxation and enjoyment.

I believe also that children should be brought up with the

rule that they do not "eat on foot." They should do their eating while sitting on a chair in the kitchen or some other appropriate place. There is no need for them to run through the house with cookies, scattering crumbs all along the way; or to touch the walls and woodwork while eating sticky candy; or to spoil the sofa and carpets by spilling food on them. It's surprising how early a child can learn this rule.

Children do spill. One mother said, "We buy four quarts of milk. Three for the children and one for the floor." It's wise to have children eat where their spilling will do the least amount of damage.

You shouldn't let your children eat oranges while sitting on the sofa any more than you would have them sleep on the kitchen table. Yet, you'd be surprised how many mothers are guilty of the former.

Now, it's easy to teach children that they shouldn't "eat on foot" if they're still young. But what should you do if your family is half grown and they have the bad habit of eating as they wander around the house? Well, there are two courses of action you could try.

One is this: Close this book and wait for the next family member who grabs a cookie and runs through the house. Then you can catch him right in the act and punish him sufficiently to make him an example for everyone. I'm afraid such action on your part would fail to get you the cooperation you want, but at least it's one idea.

Now here's the other one. If I were you, I wouldn't say a word about this new rule for several days. And then sometime when you've just served apple pie a la mode and everyone in the family is feeling right about things, you might say something like this: "You know, I've been doing some studying lately. I've been learning some new things about homemaking. I've got some wonderful suggestions for things which you can do to help me so that I, in turn, can be of more help to you. For one thing, why not do your eating sitting down in an appropriate place from now on. Then instead of having to spend so much of my time cleaning up cookie crumbs, I'll have more time to bake more cookies and prepare other goodies for you. How about it? Let's make it a rule at our house that we don't eat on foot."

Now, another thing for you to consider: I feel that clothing, pajamas, shoes, and socks should be confined to the spot (either the bedroom or bathroom) where the dressing or undressing takes place so that "picking up" can be kept at a minimum.

I've often heard women make this type of comment: "I spent the morning going through the house gathering up the dirty clothes." Really, such a thing is entirely unnecessary, and it's a waste of time. Every family member should be responsible for getting his own dirty clothes to the hamper or clothes chute. A little toddler thinks this is fun, and by the time the fun wears off, it's a habit with the older children. Now, if you need to reinforce the habit once in a while refer to the suggestions in Facet No. 12 "Grow Your Own." For instance, if the dirty clothes aren't put where they're supposed to be, they just don't get washed. I can assure you it won't be long before everyone in the family catches on and cooperates!

Remember, Mom, you're not the family doormat. Don't let your family walk all over you. Don't let them force you into slave duty. Have some practical family policies. Insist upon their cooperation and respect. They'll think more of you because of it. Your children will grow in maturity and responsibility. And your house will look lovely. There's no point in making a mess to just have to clean it up. Never forget that an ounce of prevention is worth a pound of cure.

It's a fortunate family that has a family room, or a playroom in their home where the children can romp and play and scatter toys and work on creative projects to their delight. If such a room is available, the other rooms can be generally left free to perform their specific functions. The living room, particularly, instead of appearing like a gymnasium, can be kept presentable. Then should the doorbell ring at dinnertime, bath time or right in the middle of Junior's invasion of Mars or Patty's paper-doll parade, Mother can smile with relief, realizing that even though the rest of the house is having one of those "moments" the living room is worthy of any caller.

Now, some homes are designed so the living room has to be the central hallway or the playroom. If this is the case with your home, then all you can do is your best. I know of a young mother who was living in a small apartment with two active little children. The living room was the only available place for them to play. So this enterprising mother solved the problem by sewing some rubber rings onto the corners of a large sheet. Then she placed the sheet on the living room floor and secured it by placing the rubber rings under the table and chair legs. Her children played contentedly on the sheet for hours, but then should the doorbell ring or should she want to clear the room quickly she could just roll up the sheet with toys and all and slide it from the room!

Well, I'm not sure how practical that one is. But I do know that it's a great feeling when your living room is always presentable.

In fact, I like to think of the living room like Grand-mother's memorable parlor—the place where the family's finest in furniture and decorations can be displayed in gleaming perfection and where guests can be entertained in pleasant, uncluttered surroundings. The living room can then be a place where the children enter when they are prepared to behave like little ladies and gentlemen and when they are ready to enjoy special, memory-making occasions. Because they have been taught since they were big enough to understand that they should respect property. A child can learn at a very tender age the difference between a decorative item in the house and a toy.

Remember, a wonderful aid to orderliness is a function for every room!

Second: STREAMLINE EACH ROOM.

As you are aware, much is said today about the conquering of outer space. Actually, it can also be very worthwhile and rewarding to conquer inner space! Let's talk about it.

To begin with, don't have unnecessary items around, cluttering the room, detracting from the furnishings and gathering dust. Don't overfurnish your home. To illustrate this point, consider the contrast between the display window of a variety store where many, many wares are placed, and the display window of a lovely department store where just a few articles are displayed in such a way as to enhance one another. Well, with which does your home compare? Think about it for a minute.

Another great aid to orderliness is to remove anything which doesn't add to the decorative scheme of a room. If it isn't pretty, put it away whenever possible. I don't want the window sills of my home lined with bottles of lotion and cleansers; I don't care for the counter top in my kitchen to be adorned with boxes, bottles, packages, and other assorted containers. If you allow this to happen, your kitchen will never look sparkling clean and attractive, no matter how much you scrub it.

Well, I hope your house isn't like the many houses where clutter is as permanent as the furniture. This reminds me of a cartoon I saw the other day where two little children were

watching their mother, and one child said to the other: "Someone must be coming. Mom's putting the ironing board away."

Now, if cupboard and closet space in your home isn't adequate, invest in some unfinished chests or cabinets. Some houses do have definite physical limitations, but you know, most crowded conditions can be relieved through a little ingenuity mixed with some sorting, filing, rearranging and discarding. Many women's magazines include as a regular feature clever, ingenious storage ideas. Also, helpful pamphlets about storage and good use of space are available upon request from government agencies and state universities.

Next, analyze your drawers and closets and cupboards. Place things according to how you use them. Have a reason for putting a certain item in a certain place and then KEEP IT THERE. The more consistent you are in this, the more inclined family members will be to return things to their proper places. For instance, if you return the scissors to the same spot after each use, you can be quite certain you'll always be able to locate them there. But if you put them one place yesterday and another place today, it's for sure your children will put them a third place tomorrow.

Now, another thing of great importance. Develop the PICKING UP PROCESS. Get in the habit of picking up anything out of place as you walk through your home or yard. You'd be surprised what a second spent here and there can do for the order of your home.

And speaking of the picking up process, it really means a lot to have your house "picked up" and orderly each time you go away or retire for the night. In fact, this is the best tranquilizer I know for a good night's sleep. And the next morning, your new day is a success before you've even opened your eyes.

Actually, this is such an important point that I'll take just a minute to tell you how we do it. Each evening, before our children go to bed, they are required to pick up their toys, books, papers and clothes. Then before my husband and I retire for the night, I go through the house, taking a survey of each room, and putting away anuthing that is out of place. This is the cap on the day as far as I'm concerned. It's my reward. I know my day's work is done. Then, I am ready for a good night's rest and a successful day tomorrow. I'm able to work *ahead* of myself rather than *behind* myself. And this makes all the difference in how I feel and how much I accomplish.

Now, this same picking up process can be applied whenever you leave the house for a few hours or even a few days. It's a real luxury to return to an orderly home. Instead of just trying to "get away from it all," you'll feel good about the things at home while you're away, and you'll return home feeling truly refreshed.

Third: KEEP NEAT CLOSETS AND DRAWERS.

Now that you're working toward a place for everything and everything in its place, be neat and tidy about each drawer and closet. It's well worth the second's extra time to FOLD something away instead of carelessly stuffing it in a drawer.

I hope you realize the neater you are the more space you save. Don't let things get in a mess just to take time out periodically to straighten them. "Drawer and closet cleaning time" should be just a few moments for special sorting and dusting.

Handy drawer dividers can be improvised by using small boxes such as for candy or shoes. Plastic silverware trays help keep small items in order, and plastic ice cube trays make a fine place for earrings.

I'd like to tell you about my friend, Jenny. She had a fine

husband, four lovely children, and a nice, but small home. But Jenny wasn't completely happy. She didn't really enjoy home-making and she wished she could go back to work at the office. By the way, it's been said that when a woman declares she wants to go back to work so she can give her talents to the world, what it really means many times is that at home her ironing is hopelessly behind. Well, that's the way it was with Jenny. She used to talk to me a lot about homemaking, and I discussed attitudes and scheduling with her, but nothing seemed to help.

One day I happened to be in Jenny's home on an errand. As we were visiting she asked me to look in one of her closets. Well, I hesitated because I don't make a point of looking in anyone's closets. But she insisted, and so I did. Well, I could hardly believe my eyes. You know, those cartoons of Fibber McGee closets? I hadn't known they actually existed, but here was one with everything stashed and stuffed and falling out with each opening of the door. About all I could do was laugh and say to Jenny: "No wonder you're unhappy. It would drive me crazy to live like this."

Then Jenny said, "I know. It's really getting me down. I can't find anything. We're too crowded. All I do is fight clutter. I can't go on like this any longer. And this is the day for me to change. It's my birthday. I'm thirty years old now. I figure there should be many productive years ahead of me, so I want to do some things differently from now on. Every closet in my house looks just like this. I know it's terrible, but I don't know what to do about it. I just don't know where to start. I want you to help me."

Well, I could understand her predicament. If someone handed me some crepe paper and told me to make a rose, I wouldn't know where to start. Some artistic person would have to help me. Jenny didn't have the know-how for organizing the space in her home. Now to those of you who do, the matter seems so simple you feel it's hardly worth discussing. But to the many other homemakers who don't have the knack for organizing the space in their home, they need some practical help.

In Jenny's utility closet, for instance, she was constantly irritated by the brooms and mops which fell out each time she opened the door. She had never even thought of hanging them on hooks so they'd stay in place. And besides this, they would last longer if they were kept in hanging position. And on the floor of her closet, paper bags were running loose. Think how much better it would be if all those loose bags were kept together in one large bag or container?

Jenny's utility closet was over-crowded too. She hadn't stopped to realize that much of what was in there actually belonged in the storage area.

Well, Jenny and I worked out a plan for putting her closets and cupboards in order. First, it was pointed out that sometimes in life it's necessary to take one step backward in order to go two steps forward. And in keeping with this philosophy, we realized that it wouldn't be possible for Jenny to keep up with all her usual work and clean out the closets, too. Something had to give. She would have to take one step backward in order to go forward. We decided she'd have to let the cleaning go. You know, you never get behind with the cleaning. One swipe of the cloth and the dust is gone no matter how thick it is. On the other hand, she realized that she must keep up with the meals, washing, ironing and mending. Then she secured three large boxes. One for things to throw away, another for things to give away, and another one for things to later arrange in her storage area. Then she went to work on one closet at a time.

Well, a few days later she called me to see her first closet.

I was thrilled with the results. I told her that her only mistake was that she hadn't taken a picture of the "before" and "after." Such a photo would certainly win a prize somewhere! But you know, the thing which impressed me most was not the change in the closet, but rather the change in Jenny. Her eyes were sparkling, and she was excited and interested in her home for the first time. And as Jenny made the rounds of every closet and cupboard in her home, she became a new person. She was no longer a drudge who hated housework. She was becoming a professional homemaker who was falling in love with her work.

Her attitude was positive now, and she was able to schedule her housework activities and thereby have time for her family and for herself.

Jenny's example was a profound one. There are some real reasons why it's important to keep neat closets and drawers.

Now, the fourth point: HAVE THE COURAGE TO THROW AWAY.

Be certain of an item's future value before saving it, and then put it where it belongs. Don't keep stacks of old papers, magazines, bottles, boxes, or similar items cluttered around. "When it doubt, throw it out!"

I heard of a little old lady who kept everything. People commented that she hadn't thrown away a thing in fifty years. Her only redeeming feature was that she did save things in an orderly way. After her death, a little envelope was found in her home marked: "Pieces of string too little to do anything with."

Fifth: LABEL ALL STORED ITEMS.

Items for storage should be kept in dustproof boxes or other suitable containers and should be clearly labeled as to their contents. If the items are to be stored in an attic or some other inconvenient place, it's a good idea to keep a master list of what is there. Please refer to pages 49 through 51 for an illustration of a home storage area and a copy of the master sheet.

Sixth: STORE SOME FOOD.

For convenience, and economical and security reasons, many people have a supply of food stored in their homes. Detailed information regarding what to store and how to do it can be obtained through the L.D.S. Church or your local county agricultural agency or civil defense bureau.

Specially constructed slanted shelves have proven an ideal way to store canned goods. The slant of the shelves allows the cans to roll so they are constantly rotated and turned. Compact storage space is another advantage of these slanted shelves—several dozen cases of canned goods (depending on the shelves and the sizes of the cans) can be stored in a minimum amount of space. Included in this chapter is a photograph of these shelves.

Seventh: LEARN THE FUN OF FILING.

Filing is the most systematic and successful method of taking care of papers and similar items. Besides this, filing can be lots of fun—once it gets into your blood it can be a most fascinating hobby.

Now, Here are some suggestions as to what to file:
Choice recipes—copy them on 3 x 5 inch index cards and file them in an attractive box. This enables fast finding, simplifies meal planning, and by following this method a recipe is seldom misplaced. (Manilla envelopes arranged in sequence also provide an orderly way to keep recipes.)

One time a thoughful neighbor lady brought us a delicious pie. Several days later I went to her home to thank her for it and I asked her for a copy of the recipe. She seemed pleased that I should ask, and she took me into the kitchen where she

Slanted shelves for storing canned goods.

opened a drawer which was filled with newspaper and magazine clippings. She proceeded to go through the papers until she found the recipe. It took her ten minutes. I secretly timed her just for fun! Imagine, having to go on such a recipe hunt each time you wanted to cook something.

Other things that should be filed are:

Valuable papers such as wills, deeds, mortgage papers, and insurance policies. Actually, these things should be kept in a fireproof container. They're worth more than money!

Information for income tax purposes, such as cancelled checks and receipts.

An orderly system for family statistics and records is of great value for many reasons. One of our fine friends lost her husband a year ago. In order to work out the affairs of the estate she needed a copy of their marriage license. She spent two days looking for it. You can be sure she wished for a good system at that time!

I have a file for clippings, articles, poems, thoughts, appropriate jokes, stories, and visual materials. This material—all arranged so I can find anything in a minute or so—is highly valuable in preparing talks.

Other good files such as for instructions and warranties to appliances, clothing labels and washing directions, and Christmas card names are most helpful.

We have another file for party ideas—games, decorations and favors for holiday parties, birthday parties, and bridal and baby showers.

We also have a "fun file." This is full of ideas for creative activities and fun for children for rainy days or rest time in the afternoon. Such ideas may include a recipe for play dough or finger paint, instructions for making a bubble blower, or a ten-pin game made with clothespins. This "fun file" also contains references to books and magazines which have suggestions for children's fun.

Now, one word of caution: Be very selective in the material you file and discard the rest of it in the "round file" or the waste paper basket.

As you are aware, people are always saving things, but few of them can ever find these items. I hope you're different! The secret is to keep good files. It isn't necessary to invest in expensive file cabinets; sturdy boxes can do quite nicely until you can afford the other.

There is one more type of file that I want to tell you about. It's a child's Treasure Chest. Now this treasure chest is just an empty orange box from the grocer's which is covered with each child's favorite stick-on paper. This box or Treasure Chest is actually an individual keepsake box for each child where he keeps his baby book, special papers in manila envelopes for each year of his life, selected school work, and pictures, treasures from grandparents and great-grandparents and other cherished items. Children spend many happy hours looking through their boxes and they plan how they're going to take them with them when they marry.

One mother decided to prepare some Treasure Chests as Christmas presents for her three children. She secured some appropriate boxes from the grocery store, covered them with attractive stick-on paper, and then began filling them. She said she found special papers and pictures all over the house—in closets and drawers—even under the children's beds. She said it did wonders for the order of the house and her peace of mind to get everything taken care of, and then the greatest joy came on Christmas morning as she watched her children's reaction as they discovered their Treasure Chests. No other gift pleased them so much. Carolyn said she wouldn't be surprised if someday if one of the children should write about "The Christmas I Remember Best" he wouldn't tell about the year he got a treasure chest.

Diane and her Treasure Chest.

Well, making and keeping up Treasure Chests is easy and fun to do and their value makes them one of my most worthwhile projects. Included in this chapter is an illustration of a child and her Treasure Chest. If you like this idea, maybe the illustration will be of further help to you in making some for your children.

The eighth and final item on our list is: TAKE CARE OF THE CHILDREN'S TOYS.

As you well know, toys can be a real threat to an orderly house. While children are small, have a box of adequate size for their toys. A sturdy cardboard one covered with stick-on paper makes an attractive and practical toy box. A bright, strong plastic clothesbasket also provides a good place for toys. Then as children grow older and can reach higher, drawers and shelves make ideal places for toys if you are fortunate enough to have such space.

Be sure to teach your children to help pick up their toys and put them in the container, even if it is only one toy at first. This sets a pattern; it forms a good habit.

As children reach the age where they enjoy more complex toys, (you know the kind with all the many pieces and parts to them), it is helpful to keep them in large labeled boxes, cans, or bags, separated according to type in these individual containers. For instance, place all of their puzzle pieces in one container, their construction sets in still another, and their paper dolls in a separate box. Allow your children to play with the contents of one container at a time and teach them to pick up the contents before getting another toy bag or can. Then picking up the toys becomes a part of the fun. These containers simplify the picking up process, help prevent toys from becoming broken or lost, and rotate the toys so the children don't see everything every day.

(The containers can be bags made from heavy, colorful

Toy bags hanging in children's playroom.

fabric with draw string openings. These bags help conserve space by hanging from a peg board or from hooks along a wall. Empty shortening cans, ice cream cartons, and plastic bleach bottles which have been cut away for an opening also make fine toy containers.)

Illustrations of toy bags are on page 48.

Now one last idea. A large wicker basket or cardboard drum placed on the back porch makes a good place to keep balls, bats and mitts.

Let me review the eight points for an orderly home:

1. Let each room fulfill its function.
2. Streamline each room.
3. Keep neat closets and drawers.
4. Have the courage to throw away.
5. Label all stored items.
6. Store some food.
7. Learn the fun of filing.
8. Take care of the children's toys.

It's never too late or too early. Form the orderly habit *now*. You know, if you make the things you have to do a habit you won't have to force yourself any longer. Then you will enjoy a neat home, peace of mind, and you'll be able to find things—even in the dark!

STORAGE MASTER SHEET

Top Shelf

H-1   Holiday decorations
        Valentine
        Easter
        Halloween
        Thanksgiving
H-2   Holiday decorations, Christmas
H-3   Holiday decorations, Christmas
H-4   Holiday decorations, Christmas
H-5   Holiday decorations, Christmas

Second Shelf

    C-1   Children's boots
    C-2   Children's pajamas
    C-3   Children's clothing, boys, ages 2 to 6
    C-4   Children's snowsuits, coats, jackets
    C-5   Children's clothing, girls, ages 2 to 6
    A-1   Adult's clothing, tennis and swimming

Third Shelf

    A-2   Adult's clothing, shoes, overalls, cap for painting
    B-1   Baby clothes, general
    B-2   Baby clothes, girl
    B-3   Baby clothes, boy
    S-1   Shower supplies, bridal and baby
    P-1   Party supplies, children's birthday

Fourth Shelf

    W-1   Wrapping paper, bows, boxes
    W-2   Wrapping paper, bows, boxes
    Cr-1 Creative activity supplies (cartons, paper towel tubes, etc.)
    Cr-2 Creative activity supplies (cartons, paper towel tubes, etc.)
    Cr-3 Creative activity supplies (cartons, paper towel tubes, etc.)
    Cr-4 Creative activity supplies (cartons, paper towel tubes, etc.)

Fifth Shelf and Floor

    Blankets - 1 blankets for children's play
    Blankets - 2 blankets for bedding
    Picnic basket
    Thermos
    Baby Equipment (sterilizer, infanseat, toilet seat) when not in use*
    Easter baskets*

*In large, labeled boxes or bags
to keep out dust.

Storage in basement or garage.

FACET NO. 5
MEET THE MINUTE

An ideal homemaker makes the best use of her time and energy by being efficient so that she is able not only to keep up with her housework, but she is able to be a companion to her husband and a friend and teacher to her children. She is able to pursue some personal interests which further contribute to her happiness and development.

THE MINUTE

Just a tiny little minute,
Only sixty seconds in it,
Forced upon me,
Can't refuse it,
Didn't seek it,
Didn't choose it,
But it's up to me to use it,
Give account if I abuse it.
Just a tiny little minute
But eternity is in it.

Anonymous

The poet, Robert Frost, was asked, soon after his eightieth birthday, how he managed to crowd so many interesting, important things into an unusually vital lifetime. He said, "Learn how to do the things you HAVE to do more quickly and effortlessly—save minutes—and you will gain an extra hour or more every day to do the things you really WANT to do—to see friends, listen to music, or look at pictures . . . help others in your community, civic, church, and religious activity . . . make the projects for which you're always saving plans . . . read, or perhaps even write a little poetry."

Have you ever stopped to think that frequently a poor housekeeper works twice as long as a good housekeeper because she makes work for herself? A bachelor said he had the secret to keeping house. Don't mess it up in the first place!

(Inefficient homemakers find themselves ironing a blouse while a daughter is waiting to leave for school, or a shirt while the husband is standing with his briefcase in hand. This reminds me of a poor homemaker and manager I know whose husband has never known what it's like to wear a cool shirt!)

First: MAINTAIN GOOD WORKING CONDITIONS.

To reduce steps, arrange work areas close together.

Arrange equipment so work moves in one direction.

Provide a working height suited to you and the job at hand.

Locate tools, utensils, and supplies where first used.

Store utensils and supplies that are used together in the same location.

Provide comfortable chairs and working levels for sit down jobs.

Have good light and good ventilation in all working areas.

Use work surfaces that are easy to clean and maintain.

Work clean and neatly—clean up as you go along. Don't make messes just to have to clean them up!

Second: KEEP EVERYTHING WITHIN REACH.

Arrange equipment and supplies within easy reach at center where work is done.

Use highest and lowest storage for seldom-used items.

Add step shelves, half shelves, vertical dividers, drawer dividers to make space more usable.

Have several sets of commonly used utensils and cleaning aids.

Elevate work to where it can be reached without bending. Make use of racks and small shelves on closet and cupboard doors.

Hang frequently worn clothes nearest closet door.

Have low hangers, low shelves for children's toys and clothes.

Hang frequently used equipment near place it is used.

Third: MAKE USE OF THE BEST APPLIANCES AND CLEANING AGENTS AVAILABLE.

Remember, there is only one of you. And there are lots of things. So save yourself and use things whenever you can.

To avoid bending and stretching, use long-handled tools.

Use vacuum cleaner for dusting all ledges and ridges.

Keep equipment and tools in good condition.

Use practical gadgets such as vegetable choppers, rubber scrapers, tongs, egg and tomato slicers, wire whisks, garlic presses, melon ballers, basting syringes, apple corers, and cake breakers.

For convenience in housekeeping, have such equipment as cellulose or nylon yarn mops (they don't smell sour and they don't leave water or lint on the floor) for damp mopping; floor scrubbers and wax applicators for heavy duty floor care; and long-handled brushes and squeegees for outside windows.

Adapt habits to modern time-saving tools and equipment such as automatic washers and dryers, frost-free refrigerators, kitchen disposals, dishwashers, and ironers. (Be certain in using these appliances, that you are following instructions and that the item is properly adjusted and functioning as it should. For instance, in using an automatic dishwasher, it will serve you more efficiently if you use the right kind of detergent, if your water is at the right temperature, and if the water pressure is forceful enough.)

Fourth: AVOID MAKING WORK FOR YOURSELF.

After using the mixmaster, clean it off immediately. If the batter is left on to harden, it becomes a major cleaning job to scrape and chip it off at a later date.

Put away CLEAN items in the refrigerator. Wash milk bottles or cartons that are delivered to your door—they are covered with water and ice from the truck and from sitting on the porch.

Wipe off all items before placing them in either the refrigerator or cupboard. This prevents tops sticking to bottles, it keeps anything sticky from spreading to something else, and it prevents anything dripping so as to soil a shelf. All in all, a minute's time in wiping an item off eliminates the hour's time spent in cleaning refrigerators and cupboards.

Store only covered items in the refrigerator so as to avoid spilling, spoilage, and odors.

Wipe up spilled food immediately. Particularly this is important on the range. If you KEEP a range clean, you don't have to labor nearly so long or so hard when the quarterly scouring time comes along.

Avoid being careless and sloppy; clean up as you go along. Rinse out a pan immediately after using it, and whenever it is necessary to scour a pan, place a dishcloth under it so it won't scratch the sink or counter top.

Left-over work has a tendency to multiply. Dishes become harder to wash. Clutter causes things to fall and spill; children get into more mischief, causing more clutter than ever.

It is particularly important to avoid "flitting" about the house, as is expressed by this verse:

THE OLD SAILOR

There was once an old sailor my grandfather knew
Who had so many things which he wanted to do
That, whenever he thought it was time to begin,
He couldn't because of the state he was in.

He was shipwrecked, and lived on an island for weeks,
And he wanted a hat, and he wanted some breeks;
And he wanted some nets, or a line and some hooks
For the turtles and things which you read of in books.

And, thinking of this, he remembered a thing
Which he wanted (for water) and that was a spring;
And he thought that to talk to he'd look for, and keep
(If he found it) a goat, or some chickens and sheep.

Then, because of the weather, he wanted a hut
With a door (to come in by) which opened and shut
(With a jerk, which was useful if snakes were about),
And a very strong lock to keep savages out.

He began on the fish-hooks, and when he'd begun
He decided he couldn't because of the sun.
So he knew what he ought to begin with, and that
Was to find, or to make, a large sun-stopping hat.

He was making the hat with some leaves from a tree,
When he thought, "I'm as hot as a body can be,
And I've nothing to take for my terrible thirst;
So I'll look for a spring, and I'll look for it first."

Then he thought as he started, "Oh, dear and oh, dear!
I'll be lonely tomorrow with nobody here!"
So he made in his note-book a couple of notes:
"I must first find some chickens" and "No, I mean goats."

He had just seen a goat (which he knew by the shape)
When he thought, "But I must have a boat for escape.
But a boat means a sail, which means needles and thread;
So I'd better sit down and make needles instead."

He began on a needle, but thought as he worked,
That, if this was an island where savages lurked,
Sitting safe in his hut he'd have nothing to fear,
Whereas now they might suddenly breathe in his ear!

So he thought of his hut . . . and he thought of his boat,
And his hat and his breeks, and his chickens and goat,
And the hooks (for his food) and the spring (for his thirst) . . .
But he NEVER could think which he ought to do first.

And so in the end he did nothing at all,
But basked on the shingle wrapped up in a shawl.
And I think it was dreadful the way he behaved—
He did nothing but basking until he was saved!

A. A. Milne

Some women operate just as "The Old Sailor" did. STICK TO A SPECIFIC JOB UNTIL IT IS COMPLETED. (Refer to pages 60 and 61 for suggestions as to using a cobbler apron with large pockets, a utility cart or a "step saver" to help eliminate flitting.

Fifth: ELIMINATE UNNECESSARY STEPS—AVOID "BUSY WORK."

Select clothing that doesn't require ironing, or invest in permanent press fabrics which require only a light press with the steam iron. Fold sheets, towels, and household linens without ironing. The ironing is a good place to eliminate non-essentials and thereby save time for more important activities.

Rather than large tablecloths that require fussy laundering, use place mats or vinyl or terry cloth tablecloths that need little upkeep. (The terry cloths absorb spills and save the floor, too!)

Avoid having in your home time-consuming articles to clean, such as elaborate chandeliers and Venetian blinds unless you like them so well you feel the time spent keeping them up is justified.

Sixth: DOVETAIL YOUR ACTIVITIES.

Prepare food for two meals while cooking. (Serve other half for another meal in the week or freeze it for a later date.)

Bake a double amount and freeze the other half for future use.

Use a liquid cleaning wax which will clean AND polish wood floors.

Never make two trips to town or to the store where one will do.

While washing dishes, ironing, putting up hair, or performing other routine work with your hands, use your mind by working out the next day's schedule—to be jotted down later. It's also a good idea to prepare lessons and talks for church during this time or to plan menus, parties, or other activities. These routine duties also provide an ideal time to gather your children around you for story telling, singing, reciting nursery rhymes, learning to count or saying the alphabet. As children grow older, these same opportunities may be used for visiting and talking things over.

For Mother's Day one year my husband gave me something I have wanted for a long time—a long cord for the telephone. Now I'm able to fold clothes and mend or iron while I talk. This saves much time and is a fun way to get routine jobs done. There are occasions when it's desirable to relax and just chat for a minute, but other times it can be highly helpful to a busy homemaker to work while she visits.

Seventh: WORK QUICKLY.

Because habit regulates much of what we do, smart homemakers cultivate the habit of working quickly. Then moving at a reasonably fast, consistent pace—your best pace—becomes the natural thing to do. It is much more difficult and tiring to dawdle!

The "Twenty-minute Plan" has proven successful for many homemakers. They allow themselves twenty minutes to do some task such as clearing up in the kitchen, cleaning out a closet, dusting throughout the house, or cleaning the patio. Besides being a fun game to play with yourself, the Twenty-minute Plan can do wonders for your housework.

Eighth: CONSERVE YOUR ENERGY.

Use a tray or cart to save steps and to carry heavy loads.

Whenever possible, sit down to work.

Maintain good posture in easy work positions.

To avoid stooping and reaching, place work at comfortable levels.

Push, pull, or slide heavy objects rather than lift them.

Bend at knees and hip joints instead of bending back.

Use leg muscles rather than back muscles when lifting.

Use muscles rhythmically. Each of us has a double set of muscles for accomplishing work. When they work rhythmically, one set rests while the other set works. In non-rhythmic work, both sets may operate at once. Some examples of rhythmic work in the home are: doing all the vacuuming, then all the dusting; peeling all the apples, then dicing them; cutting all the beans then snapping them.

There is no need to turn the house upside down for the weekly cleaning. This consumes too much time and energy and is frustrating. As just stated, do ALL the vacuuming, then ALL the dusting, then remove fingerprints from ALL the woodwork.

Sort laundry efficiently by improvising a partitioned clothes hamper (one side for white clothes and the other side for colored clothes), or by purchasing a special laundry sorter which consists of three heavy, unbleached muslin bags suspended from a metal frame. (See diagram.)

While working about the house, wear a cobbler-style apron with large pockets. In one pocket place items which are to be put away, in another one put things which are to be

thrown away, and in the third pocket carry a dustcloth
and a damp cloth or sponge in a plastic bag.

Another idea for efficiency in housework is to obtain a
laundry cart and convert it into a utility cart by stitching
to the inside heavy unbleached muslin to form four large
pockets and by pinning to the outside of the cart two
large bags (made from heavy muslin or pillow slips). (See
diagram below.) Label the inside pockets for various rooms
in your house, and label one outside pocket "Dirty
Clothes" and the other one "To Discard." In the cart itself
place cleaning supplies such as dustcloth, damp cloth or
sponge in a plastic bag, glass cleaner, furniture polish, and
a whisk broom and small dustpan. Then go about your
work, proceeding in a systematic, efficient manner from
room to room. Articles which you find out of place, put
in a pocket according to the room in which they belong.
Place dirty clothes and things to be thrown away in their
respective bags, and carry with you the supplies you need
as you work.

A "stepsaver" kit (milk carton carrier or plastic utility kit) serves the same purpose as a utility cart, though on a smaller scale. See illustration.

Mothers of large families find clothes sorting boxes handy. As the freshly laundered clothing is folded, the articles may be sorted into individual boxes (small ones from grocer) for each family member. This eliminates confusion as to whose stockings are whose, for example. Steps are saved as the clothing is then distributed to the closets and drawers throughout the house. See illustration.

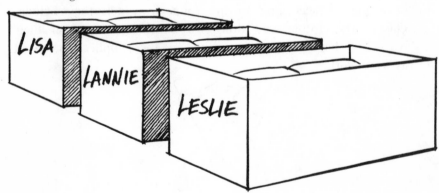

Ninth: HAVE SOME MINUTE PROJECTS.

Have a little task to do while the vegetables are boiling. you might have only a couple of minutes, but this reminds me of a story . . .

If you've ever been to New York City you have undoubtedly been impressed with that metropolis. But do you know that beneath the city are even more fascinating sights? In fact, about the only thing that won't be found is earth. A *Reader's Digest* article, published in July, 1955, stated that instead of earth you'll discover a complex jumble of cables, pipes, tunnels, and tracks. Without this nervous system, the city could not survive. There are millions of miles of pneumatic tubes to whisk Western Union telegrams around the city; almost endless miles of television circuits do a variety of jobs. Circuits for fire, burglar, and police alarms, for traffic signals and wired music make up more of this remarkable network.

There are water and sewage conduits, thousands of miles of gas pipeline, enough high pressure steam lines to heat buildings and to provide steam for pressers and Turkish baths and melt ice from sidewalks. A New York telephone worker says, "At the corner of Wall and Broad Street there isn't room to bury a pencil."

A person could spend an entire lifetime in New York without ever setting foot out-of-doors. He could live in hotels, dine in restaurants, shop in department stores, work in office buildings, all linked to the subway system by tunnels. Only at death would he have to venture on the streets—for a trip to the graveyard.

There are thousands of scheduled trains which carry millions of passengers daily.

A vast army of workers keeps the city's vital arteries functioning. Those who have the most nerve-chilling job of all are the workmen who repair the third-rail installations on the subways. Because the power cannot be shut down they must work on live rails, always within a hairbreadth of sudden death. They must work rapidly and accurately. Since some trains run on ninety second headway, THEY OFTEN HAVE ONLY THIRTY SECONDS TO SET UP, THIRTY SECONDS TO WORK, AND THIRTY SECONDS TO GET OUT OF THE WAY OF THE ONCOMING TRAIN. THIS PROCESS IS REPEATED UNTIL THE JOB IS COMPLETED.

Many people rise to success by using the minutes and seconds the average person wastes. They have learned to overcome a time leakage. An outstanding young attorney attributes much of his success to the fact that he has learned to make every minute of his day count. As a young boy he spent a summer watering the lawn of a local cemetery. It was his job to set the big rain birds at various points on the lawn. He discovered that by RUNNING from one hose to the next, he could have three minutes of extra time and during those three minute intervals he read and studied.

Those 'Extra' Moments, by Ann Wynne, *Deseret News* Homemaking Editor, Salt Lake City, Utah:

"Our success depends not only upon the use of our time," said famous newspaperman Arthur Brisbane, "but also on the use of its by-product, the odd moment."

This tip can be of golden value to a homemaker, for she invariably uses up her day fully—or thinks she does—and yet at the end wonders where it has gone and why she hasn't accomplished more.

Her only hope in keeping on top of things is in that use of the "odd moment."

It's with an odd moment that she's able to get her kitchen drawers cleaned—perhaps while she's on the phone or waiting for the soup to bubble or even while expecting a ride to come along. (Yes, drawers can be straightened even with best clothes on!)

It's while her little one is puttering in the bathtub that she gets the basin washed and the bathroom shined.

Her bed made and bedroom straightened can be done in just that odd moment before going to fix breakfast.

And a kitchen can be kept constantly clean if odd moments are used—cooking utensils washed while waiting for the family for dinner, dishwashers loaded while the last child is finishing supper.

Fifteen free minutes before lunch may be too little time to start a big job, yet plenty of time for dozens of small jobs: sweep and put order in the family room; wipe fingerprints from woodwork; tidy a kitchen cupboard; sort silverware; clean under the kitchen sink; sponge kitchen floor; sweep front and back porches or basement stairs.

Many pockets of time are empty in a homemaker's day; by putting them to swift use she can double her productivity.

These extra jobs are no more tiring than puttering around, but, oh, how joyful to be that much more on top of things at the close of day!

Goethe once wrote:

> Are you in earnest? Seize this very minute . . .
> What you can do, or dream you can, begin it,
> Boldness has genius, power and magic in it . . .

Tenth: HAVE SOME LONG-RANGE PROJECTS.

Years ago a man was concerned about finding time to move the large woodpile out by the "privy" nearer to his home. He just couldn't find the several hours it would require to do the job due to his many cares as a farmer. Finally one morning an idea occurred to him. Each time he visited the "privy" he could carry an armload of wood back to the house! Within a few weeks the woodpile had been moved— what had seemed like the impossible had been accomplished.

I know that this can be done; one summer I made three dresses—a seam a day.

By following these rules of efficiency, you will be able to save enough minutes to do not only the things you SHOULD do, but also to do the many things you WANT to do.

(P.S. Don't become an extremist in efficiency. A man complained that his wife had become so efficient that he couldn't even get up in the night for a drink of water without returning to find his bed made.)

FACET NO. 6
THE SIX "W's"

An ideal homemaker realizes that many of life's choicest blessings are gained only through hard work and therefore accepts work as a challenge and an opportunity rather than a burden.

You'll recall that we discussed THE TWO "A's" and ANOTHER "A" (Attitude, Appearance, and Ambition) as essential factors in homemaking. Here is another magic formula for success: THE SIX "W's": WORK WILL WIN WHEN WISHING WON'T!

We've talked a great deal now about the fsstest and best way to do things so as to avoid unnecessary work. Please don't misunderstand me; I'm not advocating less work so as to become idle or lazy or suggesting that you develop a disliking for work. Learn to do the required, routine work faster and better so as to have time to pursue some more creative fields of work for your joy and development and for the edification of your family and home.

Work is a great thing, as Kingsley said:

"Thank God every morning when you get up that you have something to do that day which must be done, whether you like it or not. Being forced to work and forced to do your best will breed in you temperance and self-control, diligence, and strength of will, and a hundred virtues which the idle never know."

It's true that the willing horse gets the heaviest load, but it also develops the strongest muscles and receives the most oats.

John Luther gives a valuable message in his booklet entitled, "My Blessing, Not My Doom." He says that he accidentally discovered a great bit of philosophy one time when he was on a two-month vacation. Taking such a vacation was something he had never done before and he explains why he never intends to do it again. He tells that at first everything was perfect, then an unaccountable restlessness set in—even taking the children swimming had become a chore—pleasure had lost its flavor. It wasn't until he got hold of a typewriter and began writing and working that his personal balance and peace of mind were restored.

He writes: "I've learned that I have to work in order to be happy. People need work almost as badly as they need food; without it they're devoured by restlessness and discontent.

"How many people who think they hate to work would, if they knew the truth, recognize it as the thing they most need in order to find contentment? How many people who dislike their jobs could, with a simple change of mental outlook made possible by this knowledge, enjoy their work thoroughly?

"And how many women who groan over the chores of raising a family realize later—after the children have left home—that those years were among the happiest years of all. What a pity they didn't know it in time!

"Realizing that you actually enjoy working is part of growing up. But many people never learn it; they never achieve the peace of mind and contentment this knowledge brings. They spend their lives in a prison where work is the eternal punishment.

"What is work, anyway? The fellow who goes fishing every once in a while thinks it's a great sport. The man who has to fish for a living thinks fishing is work. Which is it?

"Remember Tom Sawyer? Tom had to whitewash the

fence. But by pretending it was really fun he hornswoggled his friends into doing the job for him. And he made them pay for the privilege.

"Mark Twain, the author who created Tom Sawyer, knew what work was. 'Work consists of whatever a body is obliged to do,' said the famous humorist, 'and Play consists of whatever a body is not obliged to do.'

"Twain's definition holds the key to making any job easier and pleasanter. Work is not a concrete thing—it's a mental attitude. Nothing is either work or play but thinking makes it so.

"Whatever you do, if you do it under a feeling of compulsion, it is work. How well I remember helping the neighbors to cut the lawn, rake leaves or dry the dishes. It was fun. But the same chores at home were something else again."

How can you overcome the feeling of compulsion that makes work a burden?

YOU CAN LEARN TO DO MORE WORK AND BETTER WORK THAN YOU HAVE TO—YOU CAN DO THE BEST JOB YOU KNOW HOW—YOU CAN GO THE SECOND MILE.

The Jews, by law under the Romans, were compelled to go one mile when asked by a Roman citizen. But the Savior said, "And whosoever shall compel thee to go a mile, go with him twain." (Matt. 5:41.)

A slave is compelled to go the first mile—a free man chooses to go the second.

Many an office boy has risen to the top of his company through his efforts of going the second mile.

The housewives who dislike their work are the ones who do only the most pressing job at hand. A true homemaker puts her heart into her work and delights in doing everything she possibly can for the happiness and success of her famly.

James W. Elliott said it when he stated: "WORK is life and good WORK is good life."

That is why we should remember that work is our blessing and not our doom.

An outstanding man in our community recalls that as young farm boys he and his brothers worked hard and long to carry out the countless chores. He says that every time there was a little slack in the work, his father would decide that the corral fence needed moving and have his sons labor mightily to move it. Now as an adult, this gentleman appreciates his father's wisdom and credits the hard work he was required to do as a boy for his present status of achievement and success. He plans to make men out of his boys by having them "move corral fences."

Thomas A. Edison, the great inventor, stated:

"I am glad that the eight-hour day had not been invented when I was a young man. I am wondering what would have happened to me by now, if fifty years ago some fluent talker had converted me to the theory of the eight-hour day and convinced me that it was not fair to my fellow-workers to put forth my best efforts in my work. This country would not amount to as much as it does if the young men fifty years ago had been afraid that they might earn more than they were paid."

Nations, homes, and people progress only through hard work. As you observe around you, the men who put in only eight hours a day never really succeed financially and in serving their community; it is those who put in the extra hours who get ahead and achieve and contribute. A housewife who counts and limits her hours will never succeed, either.

She, too, must put in eight hours "and then some." She must do the essential, routine things, and also work a little harder to do more than is required to add some special touches—if she wants to be an ideal homemaker.

> Sitting still and wishing
> Makes no person great;
> The good Lord sends the fishing,
> But you must dig the bait!

FACET NO. 7

PLAN YOUR WORK
AND WORK YOUR PLAN

An ideal homemaker plans a program or a schedule for each day so that she is the master, rather than the victim, of her work.

There may be nothing wrong with you,
The way you live, the work you do,
But I can very plainly see
Exactly what is wrong with me.
It isn't that I'm indolent
Or dodging duty by intent;
I work as hard as anyone,
And yet I get so little done,
The morning goes, the noon is here,
Before I know the night is near,
And all around me, I regret,
Are things I haven't finished yet.
If I could just get organized!
I oftentimes have realized
Not all that matters is the man;
The man must also have a plan.

Douglas Malloch

Let's suppose that tomorrow morning someone is going to present you with $1,000 which you are to spend in the course of the day. You will, of course, carefully plan the expenditure of each dollar so as to get the very most from the money and be satisfied with each purchase at the close of the day.

Although it's fun to dream, it's doubtful that anyone is

going to give you $1,000 tomorrow. But you are going to receive something else of great value. Your gift will be twenty-four golden hours studded with diamond minutes and ruby seconds. These, too, you are to spend in the course of the day.

How can you get the most out of these precious hours? How can you make each minute and even every second count? How can you be pleased at the close of the day with how you've spent your time? The answer lies in budgeting your time just as you would your money.

Don't be fooled by the clock. There are only as many hours in the day as you make use of.

We all have twenty-four hours each day. Some of us do half a day's work, others a full day's work, and some people manage to do a week's work (comparatively speaking). The secret lies in ORGANIZATION.

It can be summed up this way:

> Look ahead,
> Plan ahead,
> Keep your head,
> And you'll be ahead!

Budgeting time means following a time plan or having a SCHEDULE. And an essential factor to good home management is to have a schedule. IT IS A ROAD FOR YOUR WORK TO RUN ON. There may be some detours and stop-overs, but if you intend to get anywhere you must follow a road.

Some people object, however, to having a schedule because they feel it binds and limits them. Actually, just the opposite is true. A good schedule makes you free. By using it wisely you are the master, rather than the victim, of your work.

A good, effective schedule is not an iron-clad thing. It should be workable and flexible. You must be able to adjust, to accept interruptions such as all the things children can think up, illness in the family, visitors, and occasional spur-of-the-moment activities. A schedule should lead to happiness and satisfaction, not frustration and fret.

Someone once said of a friend, "She hasn't got a schedule—the schedule's got her." Don't be guilty of this!

Don't become a slave to your home. Good housekeeping, like atomic energy, can be either edifying or destructive, depending upon how it is used. Good housekeeping, efficiency, orderliness, and organization are all means to an end—they are not the end within themselves.

PRESSURE BENT

Little Miss Gray was like her name,
She never saw the sun,
For there was always work to do,
And errands to be run.

She had no time to stop before
The park where dahlias grew,
Or listen to a thrush call,
For there were things to do.

Her feet were just a pace behind
Her body as she went,
Head forward and against the wind,
Toil-turned and pressure-bent . . .

Had she but paused to look a moment
At the pink and buttercup,
She could have had a bit of resting
And a chance for looking up!

Mary Gustafson

Several years ago I read an article in a magazine entitled, "What's a Minute More or Less?" In essence it told of a young mother who was so involved in putting a newborn baby to bed just so and right on time that she wouldn't let Grandmother, who had just come in for a quick visit, play

with the baby for a minute. A few weeks later the grandmother passed away, never again to play with the baby. The
young mother learned a valuable, but heartbreaking lesson. So
don't forget, there are times to remember, "What's a Minute
More or Less?"

There are other times, as well, when it is more sensible to
have only a very simple schedule and to let some things go.
For instance, there was a mother who, along with poor health,
had had a large family, including several sets of twins. At
times, when she was ill or when twin babies were tiny, she
had been forced to push certain activities into the background
for several months at a time. She was wise enough to realize
that it was more important to have clean baby bottles than to
have clean windows. The sad part, however, is that this good
mother was severely criticized by some of her neighbors for
not keeping the house as spick-and-span as they thought she
should. The neighbors should have recalled that the mother
HAD BEEN a good housekeeper and should have had the
confidence and understanding that she WOULD BE AGAIN,
but that she currently was being a good mother. If circumstances should cause a temporary conflict between being a
good homemaker and being a good housekeeper, it is most
commendable when a woman is able to place first things first.

A schedule wisely used, however, is a "goal mine," and a
goal mine is a "gold mine!"

Parkinson once stated: "Work expands so as to fill the
time available for its completion." I heard a young mother
bear out this truth when she said, "I can do the work in an
hour if I have to which otherwise can consume the whole
morning."

Another young wife spent the entire morning washing the
breakfast dishes—because she claimed she had nothing else to
do.

Keep your eye on the clock as you work. Set imaginary goals or deadlines, if you don't have any actual ones. This adds a challenge to your work and helps you to move consistently at your best speed. It also helps to avoid the seeming endlessness of a job. For instance, set a time for washing the dishes, ironing a shirt, peeling the potatoes, and so forth. Meeting your goals and deadlines offers a sense of satisfaction and accomplishment. Time yourself on some of the duties that seem a little monotonous to you. It's invigorating to find out that it takes only two minutes to clear the table instead of the twenty minutes you thought it did. Once you know how long it takes, it doesn't take so long!

Don't just spin your wheels! A schedule helps prevent this.

In planning your schedule, it is a good idea to consider people you know and see who overdo and who underdo, and then select someone who has found a happy medium, who can be an ideal and an inspiration to you and who does things as you would like to. Then observe how she manages.

Next in planning a schedule, classify jobs as to their importance and urgency. Place first things first; such as first the needs and companionship of your husband and children; second, home duties; and third, outside activities. Where organization is used, however, a great deal can be accomplished and under normal circumstances there will be time for all three phases in a homemaker's life.

Then take several minutes to plan the next day. You may run through your mind the routine duties as well as any extra or special activities that you know are coming up. Decide the order in which you want to do them and the best method with which to work. Allow some time also for the unexpected incident which is certain to happen. By planning what you want to do at least a day in advance, you'll discover that nearly double the amount of work can be accomplished. (One

lady had so much to do, she didn't know where to begin. So she decided to take a nap and get that over with first!)

Let's go through a specific schedule together. This is how I manage our home—you may wish to do things differently. THE IMPORTANT THING IS TO HAVE A SCHEDULE.

First, have a DAILY schedule. Every day I make the beds, clean up and sweep the kitchen, clean the bath fixtures and the bathroom floor, wash and fold a batch or two of clothes, take out the garbage, pick up throughout the house (this goes on continuously), prepare the meals, and care for and train our children. (Please refer to Facet No. 12 for suggestions regarding children's chores.)

On Mondays and Wednesdays I also dust throughout the house, dust mop the floors, shake the scatter rugs, sweep porch and walks, vacuum in vital areas, and keep up the ironing and mending. (I mend many articles while talking on the phone.) The articles which require ironing I mend as I iron. I consider these heavier days. By following such a program I still have time for unexpected activities and frequently there is an extra hour or so for myself.

Tuesdays and Thursdays are lighter days when, in addition to the daily routine, I include baking, outings, playing with children, appointments, and free time for myself to work on special projects such as writing this book.

Secondly, have a WEEKLY schedule. I shop once a week (usually on Friday). I clean the house thoroughly once a week (usually on Saturday) and I prepare as much food as possible for Sunday. (If the children are not able to help me with the cleaning and cooking, however, I do some of the heavy cleaning another day of the week.) Then on Sunday we attend church meetings, prepare lessons, study, and read, and have our Family Hour. I enjoy a complete change from the six-day routine on Sunday. Then by Monday I feel refreshed and consequently have a better week.

Third, have a MONTHLY schedule. Once a month, I clean the baseboards and other ridges throughout the house, do an extra thorough cleaning of the overstuffed pieces, clean mirrors, picture frames, lamp shades, and light bulbs. I wash the windows that are dirty, mop and wax all floors (including our rumpus room floor), wash scatter rugs, and clean any closets, cupboards, or drawers necessary.

Each Friday as I do the regular cleaning, I include several of these cleaning projects so that by the end of the month all are completed and no one day is over-loaded.

Fourth, have a QUARTERLY schedule. Several times a year I do a thorough cleaning of the range (to keep grease spattering at a minimum, see "broiling hint" on page 95) and refrigerator. I polish the furniture. (A reliable furniture store can advise you as to a good brand of polish.) Fingerprints which appear in the meantime can be buffed away with a soft cloth. Once a year the old wax should be removed by using a cloth or sponge slightly dampened in clear water. Buff dry.) I also sort the seasonal clothing at this time. I work these special projects in on some of those lighter days.

Finally and fifth, have a SEMI-ANNUAL schedule. Twice each year, usually in the spring and fall, I really clean house. This includes everything from polishing the silverware to cleaning the draperies and walls. (The details regarding this will be covered under FACET No. 9, HOW TO CLEAN HOUSE.)

William James said, "Nothing is so fatiguing as the eternal hanging-on of an uncompleted task." Carrying out this schedule I'm suggesting isn't nearly the work that worrying about the jobs is!

I've found that the most beneficial act in putting this schedule into operation is to GET AN EARLY START. It's an excellent idea to sleep no longer than necessary and then to

SUGGESTED SCHEDULE

Daily

make beds
clean up and sweep kitchen
clean bath fixtures and floor
wash and fold a batch or two of
clothes
take out the garbage
pick up throughout the house
prepare the meals
care for and train children

Monday and Wednesday

dust furniture throughout the house
dry mop floors and vacuum where
necessary shake scatter rugs
iron and mend

Tuesday and Thursday

bake
time for self for:
appointments
visiting
special projects

Friday

change linen on part of beds
plan menus and shop

Sunday

attend church meetings
read and study
Family Hour

Saturday

(if you have some helpers. If not,
schedule some of the cleaning for
another day)
change linen on rest of beds

clean house thoroughly:
vacuum carpet and
overstuffed pieces
dust   water plants
remove finger prints around
doorways and light switches
mop kitchen and bathroom
wax (when necessary)
also include one of the following:

first Saturday of the month

dust baseboards, ledges

second Saturday of the month

extra thorough vacuuming of overstuffed sofa and chairs, clean mirrors picture frames, lamp shades,
light bulbs

third Saturday of the month

wash windows if necessary

fourth Saturday of the month

mop and wax all floors
wash scatter rugs if necessary

fifth Saturday of the month

clean any closets, cupboards,
and drawers necessary
cook and bake for Sunday
family outing or other activity

Quarterly

polish furniture   clean range
defrost (if necessary) and clean refrigerator
sort seasonal clothing

Semiannual

spring and fall house cleaning

arise as soon as you awake. An extra hour's work before breakfast time can set the day running so smoothly that nearly double the amount of work can be accomplished than if you start out behind. Remember: "An ounce of morning is worth a pound of afternoon," and we read in Poor Richard's Almanac, "He that riseth late must trot all day, and shall scarce overtake his business at night."

✳ Another important phase of organization is in regards to shopping and meal planning. Good planning can save both time and money here. It is a good idea to keep a slip of paper handy during the week to "add to" as you run out of items or think of things you need to buy. Then before shopping, take an inventory of your supplies and add anything else to the list that is needed. Plan your menus (at least the main dishes and desserts) for the week, with the aid of newspaper ads and your recipe file. (List these menus in your agenda book or calendar—see page 87—as you do so.) Write down on your shopping list any ingredients you must buy. This way you seldom forget anything and you don't overbuy.

If planning meals a week in advance sounds difficult to you, begin by planning two or three meals in advance and increase the number until you can plan a week ahead.

A woman confided that she has never served a meal on time in the seven years of her marriage. She says sometimes dinner has been two or three hours late. This is a source of serious annoyance to her husband and causes her to feel inadequate and unhappy as a homemaker. A little system such as the following one has helped her: (The term "on time" does not necessarily mean that you must eat at precisely the same hour every day—the time may vary slightly from day to day. It means, rather, that all the food should be prepared and ready to be served at the same time and at the time the family is ready to eat.)

1. Plan the menu in advance and have all the food items and ingredients in the house.

2. Begin preparations in an orderly kitchen—all evidence from the previous meal should have been cleared away.

3. Appoint a time when the meal should be served and then work backwards in timing with the clock so everything will be ready at the same time. If necessary, write a schedule and follow it to the minute until such planning becomes routine and automatic.

4. Learn to do several things at once. For instance, while you are keeping an eye on the vegetables which are cooking or the meat that is broiling, set the table or toss a salad.

Now, being organized well enough to serve meals on time is not enough. There is lots more to being a good cook. Here are some more suggestions in four points:

1. Serve hot things hot and cold things cold. A really good cook makes a special point of this.

2. Make certain your meals are well balanced. For instance, don't serve too many carbohydrates at one meal and forget the proteins.

3. Have a variety from one meal to another. Even if it is your favorite recipe, don't serve it too often. Keep alert to new recipes and check your files once in a while. Revive an old favorite dish.

4. Take pride in serving food attractively. It tastes better that way. (Remember, the eye is the first to feast.) Use attractive place mats or table cloths; use matching dishes and silverware (even inexpensive ones can match); keep the color of food in mind as you plan menus, and add some creative touches to your table service.

Being a good cook doesn't necessarily involve lots of money and time; it's a matter of know-how.

In entertaining or preparing dinner for guests, good managing is essential if you want to have delicious food served on time, have a presentable home, and if you are to be a calm, gracious hostess. Shop and clean PRIOR to the day of the party, prepare as many foods as possible in advance, and do not leave anything until the last minute except that which cannot possibly be done earlier.

A schedule—or a program—can work for you if you really WANT it to. If you look for excuses, you'll find them. But if you are determined to make it succeed, you can. If your schedule fails the first day, try again and again. Each time you do so you'll find that you can be just a little more effective in carrying it out. Then it won't be too long before you will be enjoying the countless benefits and advantages that a good schedule, wisely used, offers. You'll find by getting your work down to a system, along with applying the skills and hints regarding orderliness and efficiency (FACETS NO. 4 and 5), that there is enough time. You will also discover that by following a schedule and doing today's work today, you will enjoy a rare feeling among homemakers—that of being caught up with your work. And a schedule, instead of wearing you down, will give your life new zest.

Remember, "It's better to plan too much and get only half of it finished than to plan nothing and get it all done!"

AN AID TO MEMORY

There is no point in having a schedule unless you can remember it. Plans can be carried out only if you remember to do so. Everyone should develop some sort of "an aid to memory," whether it be a string around her finger, a calendar that can be marked, a kitchen blackboard, or some other method.

Calendars and blackboards are good for coordinating family messages and activities, but for my personal management, I prefer an appointment book because of the space it offers for appointments and notekeeping, it is personal, I can plan far in advance with it, it can't be accidentally erased, and it's small enough that I can carry it with me in my handbag.

Successful businessmen use such a book, and since running a home is really big business (in many aspects), an appointment book can also help a homemaker to be more successful.

After the initial cost of buying a binder, the fillers can be obtained for a nominal fee each year. The amount of money involved is more than compensated by the innumerable advantages an appointment book offers.

An appointment book prevents cluttering the mind. As soon as an item is written down, you needn't worry about it anymore—it is almost as good as done. Instead of scattered and easily lost notes written on backs of envelopes or on slips of paper, this keeps everything intact and eliminates much wonder, worry, and frustration, and serves as a budget book as far as time is concerned. It keeps you from forgetting important appointments, birthdays, and special things to do. It helps you to carry out your intentions and overcome procrastination; it helps you to apply yourself and thereby accomplish things instead of just puttering; it helps you avoid last minute frenzies; and as Will Rogers said, "It keeps yesterday from using up too much of today." All in all, in this jet-propelled age, such a book can prevent one's having a nervous breakdown trying to keep track of all the details of an involved life.

May I tell you how I use my book?

My book is divided into sections. Let's first discuss the diary or day-to-day section. On the left side of the page where the hours of the day are listed, I write any appointment I might have or anything which must be done at a specific time.

Once a week, just before I go marketing, I list the menu for each dinner for that coming week. (I list this about 5:30 each day which is the time we generally eat.) Then early each day I check the menu so I have frozen items thawing and all preparations made. This way dinner can be served on time with the least amount of worry and difficulty.

I have found it a helpful idea to write (in red pencil or ink) birthdays and anniversaries which I want to remember at the top right hand corner of each page. (At the beginning of a new year I go through my agenda book and list these occasions.) This way it's easy to send cards or make calls when best wishes are in order.

On the right side of the page I list the tasks or activities in order of importance which I would like to accomplish during the day. By now I can remember routine duties without listing them although as a young bride I wrote them down! This list is just for special activities, or for tasks which consume enough time that planning for them is important. If, for instance, I want to bake a cake or do something for an ill neighbor, I list it for Tuesday (unless it is an emergency, then everything is dropped to give prompt help); perhaps certain letters must be written on Thursday; on Saturday we promised to take the children on an outing; and on Sunday I plan to prepare a lesson I teach in one of our church auxiliaries. I never have to wonder what to do next and every minute is put to use.

Also, I make a note of any phone calls I should make that day or during the week, then I don't have to take time trying to think whom I was to call, and in this way I seldom fail to make all necessary calls—ranging from ordering hamburger buns at the bakery to thanking someone for a special kindness. (A reproduction of a page from this agenda book is included in this chapter.)

For me, this little book means accomplishment and peace of mind. It saves embarrassment, disappointment and serious mistakes—and it is such fun to check items off as they are

completed! I have a friend who writes things down even after she's done them just to be able to cross them off!

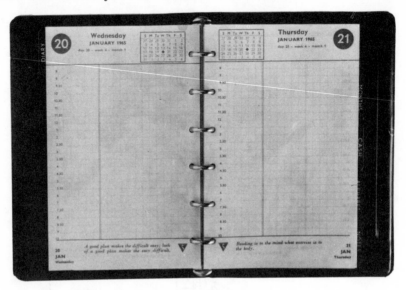

Seven Star Diary — Order from Deseret Book Company, 44 E. South Temple, Salt Lake City, Utah 84110

Charles Schwab, one of the first presidents of Bethlehem Steel Company, once inquired of efficiency expert Ivy Lee: "If you can give us something to pep us up to do the things we know we ought to do, I'll gladly pay you anything within reason you ask."

"Fine," answered Lee. "I can give you something in two minutes that will step up your 'doing' by at least fifty per cent."

"All right," said Mr. Schwab. "Let's have it."

Mr. Lee handed Mr. Schwab a blank sheet of note paper and said: "Write down the six most important tasks you have to do tomorrow and number them in the order of their importance. Now, put this paper in your pocket and the first thing tomorrow morning look at item one and start working on it until it is finished. Then tackle item two in the same way; then item three and so on. Do this until quitting time.

"Don't be concerned if you have only finished one or two. You'll be working on the most important ones. The others can wait. If you can't finish them all by this method, you couldn't have with any other method either; and without some system, you'd probably not even have decided which was the most important.

"Do this every working day. After you've convinced yourself of the value of this system, have your men try it. Try it as long as you wish and then send me a check for what you think it is worth."

A few weeks later Mr. Schwab sent Ivy Lee a check for $25,000 with a letter saying the lesson was the most profitable he had ever learned.

In five years, this plan was largely responsible for turning the unknown Bethlehem Steel Company into the biggest independent steel producer in the world. And it helped to make Charles Schwab one hundred million dollars.

This can work for you! Try it! It could revolutionize your life.

Now, back to the agenda book ...

At the beginning of each new month is a blank page. Here I list the special projects for the month and then work them in on those light days I spoke of, or whenever I have an extra minute. Of course, there is sometimes some juggling that must be done as unexpected things arise, but this serves as a goal to work for. Usually I can look back over a month, pleased to see that such things as a certain baby book was brought up to date, our summer clothes were put away for the season, a new dress was made, or a certain book was read.

In the next section are a number of blank pages. On these I write notes to myself. One page contains a list of household and personal items I want to buy as I can afford them. Sometimes by the time I can afford a certain thing, I find that I don't really need it after all, and thereby save lots of money! On the other hand, often I still want the item and this list helps me buy one or two things a month.

I keep similar lists concerning my husband and children and my parents and other relatives. At birthday and Christmas times, these lists offer excellent gift suggestions.

On another page I keep notes for baby books and family records which I enjoy transcribing periodically throughout the year.

One list contains names of friends we would like to visit. Perhaps they have recently moved into a new home or have had a baby or for some reason we would like to call on them. Occasionally on a Saturday or Sunday afternoon we'll look over the list and visit several people in one area of the valley.

Another page contains names of people we would like to invite to dinner or otherwise entertain in our home. We enjoy using this list whenever we can.

On still another page are listed special places of interest we'd like to visit. For instance, last summer we planned to take our children to the zoo, the dairy, and to visit the Pioneer Memorial Village. Such a list gives one something to work for—otherwise the visit can be put off until it never is accomplished. Only by planning for the time, working for the time, and taking the time will you get things done.

There is also an alphabetized section where I keep addresses and phone numbers.

This is just an idea of what is in my little brown book. It is one of my favorite possessions. As far as I'm concerned, this book is a valuable key to happiness and satisfaction in the innumerable activities of homemaking.

A wise man once said that every person should carry with him two books: one in which to read and one in which to dream. This agenda book is my book of dreams. And, as we are told in the song "Happy Talk" from South Pacific, "You've got to have a dream. If you don't have a dream, how're you going to have a dream come true?"

FACET NO. 8
TRY THE OLD WAYS — TRY THE NEW

An ideal homemaker is prepared to perpetuate
the good things she learned in her own home
and is ever alert to new ideas and hints which
will make her work more effective and help
her to be an increasingly better homemaker.

The daily newspaper, magazines, booklets, neighbors, and mothers are fine sources of "Hints for the Homemaker." It's a good idea to make a file or indexed scrapbook of practical ideas for future reference. Here are a few to start you in your collection:

CHILD CARE

Iron color transfers on the front of cotton underclothes to aid the children in dressing themselves.

Rub sandpaper lightly over the soles of baby's new shoes before you put them on him, and he won't slip and fall quite so easily or so often while learning to walk.

To aid a child in getting his shoes on the right feet, trace an outline of his shoes on a piece of paper. Have him place his shoes over the traced outline so that they fit exactly. Then as he steps into his shoes they will be correctly positioned for left and right feet.

Form a "child-pool" with other willing mothers and rotate toddlers around the neighborhood several hours a week. This is lots of fun for the children and enables the mothers to have a few free hours occasionally in which to accomplish work without their "help."

CLEANING

A little vinegar added to a bucket of cold water will clean

a linoleum floor without removing the wax.

(For other cleaning hints, see FACET NO. 9.)

COOKING AND BAKING

To keep grease spattering at a minimum when broiling meat, consult a reliable chart to determine the distance the broiling rack should be from the heat and the length of broiling time. Place a little water in drip pan to prevent grease from burning, and if your range is electric, broil with the door three inches ajar. For easier cleaning of the broiling rack and drip pan, leave them in the warm oven covered with wet paper toweling during the course of the meal.

Before frosting a cake, glaze it with a thin paste of powdered sugar and water to prevent crumbs getting into the frosting.

For a neat cake plate, cover the edge of the plate with triangular shaped pieces of waxed paper and then place the cake on the plate and frost it. After the cake is frosted, carefully pull the papers away.

Brush the top of your pie crust with milk before placing it in the oven and the crust will turn a golden brown.

To sour milk for baking purposes, add two tablespoons of vinegar to one cup of sweet milk and stir.

To tint coconut, fill a glass jar not more than half full of coconut, add a few drops of diluted food coloring and shake. For toasted coconut, spread a thin layer of coconut on a baking sheet and place it in a moderate oven. Stir frequently to insure even browning.

If you have over-salted the soup, boil a slice of raw potato, in it for a short time. Then remove the potato, which will have absorbed much of the salt.

To distribute raisins, currants, and other fruits evenly throughout your cakes, dust them first with flour before mixing them into your batter.

To prevent a fruit pie from boiling over while in the oven, insert several little "smoke stacks" of macaroni or pieces of drinking straws in the crust.

Arrange spices in alphabetical order on shelf for easier finding.

Store flour sifter in plastic bag to prevent flour spilling in the cupboard or drawer.

To cut down on the dishwashing at baking time, keep extra measuring cups and spoons in your cannisters.

Frozen meat will thaw out in practically no time if you sprinkle over it the amount of salt needed for seasoning. This is expecially helpful for ground meat that you want to shape into patties or a meat loaf.

Walnuts will not turn rancid if you put them in a plastic bag and freeze them.

A half teaspoon of bacon drippings or other grease added to the water in which sweet potatoes are boiled will keep that hard-to-remove substance from forming on the sides of the pan. This same trick works with other root vegetables.

Before molding a salad, rinse the mold in cold water, then grease it with salad oil. When set, the salad will leave the mold without sticking, and the oil gives it added luster.

Place a pan of water in the bottom of the oven when you reheat rolls and biscuits. The steam from the water will rise and make the bread taste fresh and it will be as soft as the day it was baked.

If you don't want to heat the oven just to warm a few light rolls for dinner, put them in the top part of your double boiler, over water, and heat them over one of the burners.

Cut a thin slice (about the size of a half dollar) from the bottom of a grapefruit or cantaloupe and it won't wobble and skid on the plate.

When cooking and eating out-of-doors, rub a bar of soap over the bottom of your pots and pans before using them over an open fire. Come clean up time, the smoke stains will vanish with the bubbles.

HOUSE MAINTENANCE

After painting a room, set a bucket of water in it and the odor will go away more quickly.

To restore a neglected paintbrush, soak it in hot vinegar.

Whenever you do any painting around the house, fill an empty nail polish bottle with some of the left-over paint. The small brush is just the right size for touching up the chips and scratches that will inevitably appear.

Touch up old or worn furniture and carpets with fabric spray paint or Rit dye.

It's safe to drive a nail into a plastered wall if you will first put a strip of cellulose tape over the spot and drive the nail through it.

For an inconspicuous mending job on sheer curtains, apply a bit of colorless nail polish and press the torn edges together with your fingers.

Small rugs placed over your carpet will help to keep the carpet clean, but if they have hard backs, they will also cause the carpet to wear faster by creating friction as you walk.

Plastic or cellophane covers left on lamp shades actually do more harm than good. Dust filters in, causing streaks on the shade. (Lamp shades are kept covered in stores to protect them from finger prints until they are sold, but they are frequently unwrapped, dusted, and recovered.)

LAUNDRY

Stuffed animals and dolls look almost as good as new after a good wash and fluff in an automatic washer and dryer. (Make certain, however, that the colors are fast and the seams are secure!)

To remove the soiled line on collars and cuffs, use a degreasing agent (good ones are available on the market). This removes the soil more quickly and is easier on the fabric than a brush.

When putting a new cover on your ironing board, first dip it in cold starch and then tack it firmly in place. As it dries, it shrinks, leaving a smooth, taut surface that won't stretch and wrinkle the first time you iron on it. Also, the starch will keep it from getting soiled very easily, so it won't need changing quite so often.

MISCELLANEOUS

To prevent silver salt and pepper shakers and other silver pieces from tarnishing, store them in air-tight containers such as plastic bags tied with an elastic.

When giving a home permanent, help the short locks around the hair line to have a tight curl by winding them on a white pipe cleaner which has been dipped in the permanent solution. (Pipe cleaners also make good curlers for little girls who don't have much hair.)

My grandmother had a wise philosophy. She said, "Before your husband comes home, have the table set. The psychological effect is remarkable; he'll think dinner is nearly ready (though it may not be) and will contentedly sit down with the newspaper."

Refer frequently to your collection of hints and use some of the good ideas you find. In homemaking it is essential to be progressive. Keep up-to-date. Know the quality brands of soaps, cleaners, and foods. Read current articles in publications on good homemaking suggestions. Collect and use good recipes. Be willing to experiment a little. It is fun to be adventuresome.

"A man's age can be determined by the degree of pain he feels when he comes in contact with a new idea." How old are you?

FACET NO. 9

HOW TO CLEAN A HOUSE— HOW TO KEEP IT CLEAN

An ideal homemaker is consistent in applying the best skills and methods she knows. She has a built-in self-starter.

One example of consistency in homemaking lies in cleaning a house and keeping it clean. Let's discuss the deep, extra thorough type of cleaning which may either be spaced throughout the year or done each spring when the furnace is turned off and the air becomes cleaner.

In regards to this heavy cleaning, some system is better than none, and some systems are better than others. Here's one I would suggest.

Instead of it being a time of great upheaval with rugs rolled up, the furniture in the middle of every room throughout the house, tables covered with everything but food, and general havoc prevailing, it can be a time of satisfying, orderly accomplishment.

The first important step is to secure as many modern labor-saving devices and supplies as you actually need, or prepare by yourself some of the time-tested, economical cleaning aids. Here is a double list of both commercial and homemade products. An item from either list will do a particular job well. You don't have to have money to be clean!

Keep in mind that several light cleanings are easier on the surface or material to be cleaned than are fewer harsh cleanings.

COMMERCIAL PRODUCT	HOMEMADE PRODUCT
chemically treated dustcloth	soft rag (rinsed in mild vinegar solution and then dried.)
chemically treated floormop	soft rag (treated in vinegar as above) over broom or mop
all-purpose cleaner for wood-work, painted walls	solution of: one gallon warm water, one cup sudsy ammonia, one-half cup vinegar, one-fourth cup sal soda (wear gloves.) (If walls have a sheen on them which you want retained, eliminate the sal soda.)
cleanser for porcelain	flannel cloth sprinkled with salt or baking soda
upholstery and carpet shampoo	detergent suds
glass and mirror sprays	solution of vinegar and water (polish with crumpled newspaper.)
wallpaper cleaner	stale chunks of bread, rubbed over wallpaper in even, vertical strokes remove soiled spots (stale bread crumbs also clean picture portraits)
wax remover self-polishing floor wax paste wax for wood floors	add a little packaged water softener to hot soap suds and work with a scrubbing brush
oven cleaner steel wool soap pads stainless steel pads oven protector (silicone spray)	ammonia and water (see page 105)
copper cleaner	dip half a lemon in salt and rub the object. Rinse in hot water and polish with a soft cloth

aluminum cleaner

hot soapy water plus a thorough rinse in scalding water. (If pan is discolored, boil rhubarb or tomatoes in it to remove stain.)

silver polish

place silverware in an aluminum pan and fill with a gallon of hot water to which one table-spoon of salt and one teaspoon of soda have been added. Swish silver around for several minutes, rinse well and polish with a soft cloth.

ceramic tile cleaner

sponge dipped in ammonia solution

drain cleaner (consult your plumber regarding what to use and how often to do so.)

moth and mildew sprays

scratch concealer

for dark woods, dye the scratches with iodine (Repeat applications until scratch disappears.)

for light woods, rub the scratched area with the cut sur-face of walnut or Brazil nut meat

for natural woods, treat the scratched area with mineral oil

furniture polish

homemade furniture polish:

1 part Boiled Linseed Oil
5 parts *Odorless* Mineral Spirits
(available through paint stores)

mix in glass or metal container. Apply to furniture with a soft cloth and then buff with another soft cloth. Dispose of the solution and rags after each use because they are flammable.

to *clean* and polish furniture (furniture pieces which are fingerprinted; sticky, dirty paneling or varnished kitchen cabinets):
1 quart hot water (as hot as you can touch it)
3 Tb. Boiled Linseed Oil
1 Tb. turpentine
work quickly while the water is still hot. (When the water cools, the solution makes the furniture gummy.) Mix in disposable glass or metal container. Apply to furniture or cabinets with a soft cloth and then polish with another soft cloth. Dispose of solution and rags when finished.

rubber spray for scatter rugs

sew canning jar rings on reverse side of rug

to clean knotty pine walls, use a solution of one-half cup ground glue (available at paint stores) and a pail of warm water (This will give the wood a brilliant lustre and will protect it from finger prints. The solution washes off with the next cleaning.)

vacuum cleaner with accessories

electric floor scrubber and polisher

sponge or absorbent cloth

When in doubt about the care or upkeep of any particular item in your home, contact the manufacturer, a sales representative, or your county agricultural agent.

After assembling the needed equipment, the second step is to clean the house!

Two schedules are suggested—take your choice according to your needs and helpers at the moment.

1. Attempt only one room at a time and plan to spend from a day to approximately a week on it, depending upon its size. A small bathroom might take a day. A large kitchen could require most of a week. Following this method prevents the entire house from being turned upside down; enables you to keep up the meals, the washing, and the light, routine cleaning of the other rooms. This type of schedule also allows some time for you to pursue other interests so you won't feel completely bogged down in your battle against dust and soil. With such a program, the average home can be thoroughly cleaned in a month's time.

2. But if you LIKE to turn everything upside down, work like a demon from dawn until midnight, and get it all over with in three to six days—why, go ahead and do it! If you have someone to help you for a few days, this is the way!

Because the kitchen is usually the most difficult room to clean, let's begin there with this suggested plan of attack:

I KITCHEN
    A. Cupboards—special project for one day.
        1. Empty and wash.
        2. Sort food products—throw away any item that looks the least bit suspicious of being spoiled.
        3. Dust and wash dishes.
        4. Give pots and pans their beauty treatment using commercial or homemade cleaning aids.

5. Replace shelf paper if necessary.
6. Replace dishes, foods, and pots and pans. (Be certain to place the foods you've had the longest nearest to the front and your most-used dishes and pans at the front and on the handiest shelves.)

B. Range and oven—another day's project.
1. Soak removable parts from range and oven overnight in bathtub partially filled with water and a little ammonia.
2. Put a spray attachment on your ammonia bottle. Just before going to bed, spray your oven walls. Close the oven door. The next morning wipe the interior of the oven with steel wool pads and the crusted grease will come off like magic. (Caution: do not breathe fumes while spraying.)
3. OR clean oven with commercial oven cleaner.
   a. Use steel wool pads to remove stubborn deposits.
4. Rinse thoroughly.
5. Spray with one of the new products which helps keep an oven clean.
6. Clean around elements by using steel wool pads.
   a. To clean a built-in stainless steel model, a special stainless steel cleaner is available.
   b. To clean a gas range, remove the burners and scrub them with a stiff brush in hot suds. (A pipe cleaner injected into flame outlets will remove any deposits collected there. Foreign material collected in burner throat may be cleaned with a narrow brush.)
7. Clean exterior of the range by washing with a detergent suds or all-purpose cleaner and a soft cloth or sponge.
8. Rinse and wipe dry.

a. A wax finish may be given by using the new cleaning waxes especially adapted for enamel.

C. Refrigerator—even the nonfrosting or self-defrosting models need a thorough periodic cleaning.

    1. If yours does require defrosting, turn control to "Off" or "Defrost."

    2. Remove food.

       a. Wrap frozen items in newspaper.

    3. Remove ice trays.

    4. A blunt tool, such as a wooden paddle, can be used to scrape the frost from the walls.

    5. Remove and wash shelves and other accessories.

    6. After the frost has completely melted, empty the drip tray and wash it.

    7. Thoroughly wash the interior of the refrigerator, using a sponge or cloth and a solution of three tablespoons baking soda to a quart of water. (Soda water removes any refrigerator odors which might be lurking.)

    8. Wash the rubber or plastic gasket surrounding the door with soap, not detergent.

    9. Rinse and dry the gasket.

    10. Turn control up and replace items.

    11. Clean the exterior as you did the range. (See B 7 and 8.)

D. Ventilating fans.

    1. Brush and clean filter and any other removable parts.

    2. Clean exterior with a damp cloth.

    3. Remove fuzz from blades with the vacuum cleaner crevice attachment.

E. Walls and woodwork—be certain before attempting to wash the walls that the paint is washable.

    1. Begin at the bottom of the wall and work up, using a sponge or a soft cloth. (Proceeding from bottom to top prevents dirty water from dribbling down and streaking the walls.)

        a. Clean only a small area at a time and work in a circular motion.

        b. Rinse each area before continuing.

    2. Complete the room by washing ceiling.

F. Windows—next on the agenda.

    1. Wash, using either a commercial or homemade cleansing solution.

    2. Polish with a soft cloth or crumpled newspaper.

G. Sink—routine upkeep by the use of good detergents and scouring when necessary (followed by a thorough rinsing) should keep the sink free from stains and grease.

    1. Should a stain need to be removed, fill the sink with water to which one-fourth cup bleach has been added and let soak until the stain can be removed.

H. Curtains

    1. Wash according to type of fabric.

    2. Starch if necessary.

    3. Iron if necessary.

I. Floors

    1. Clean by using an all-purpose floor cleaner or mild suds.

    2. Remove old wax if necessary.

    3. Rewax with self-polishing wax. (Caution: select wax which is shiny but not slippery.)

        a. A waxed floor is easier to keep up—even a broom glides over it with less effort.

        b. A shiny (no slick) floor is more pleasing to walk on.

        c. There is something about a shiny floor which

tends to make a house look sparkling clean all over.

II LIVING ROOM

A. Curtains and drapes
1. Remove loose dust with vacuum cleaner and take down from wall.
2. Wash or clean according to type of fabric.
3. Press if necessary.
B. Fireplace
1. Scrape off excess soot.
2. Remove ashes from ash bin and soot which you have previously loosened.
3. Clean hearthstone and stone or brick around outside of fireplace. (Consult manufacturing firm regarding the cleaning method to be used for your particular stone or brick. Inquire also about a sealer which can be used to protect the hearthstone. In fact, the manufacturer will clean the stone or brick work and seal the hearthstone for you for a nominal fee.)
4. Polish andirons, screen frame, and other equipment. (Lighter fluid will do an effective job of polishing these items.)
5. A darkened screen can be restored by spraying it periodically with a metallic-colored paint.
C. Take down pictures, ornaments, and books.
1. Dust thoroughly.
D. Move the furniture away from the walls.
E. Clean walls.
1. If they are only dusty, they may just require dusting with a clean cloth over a broom or clean dry mop, or going over with the dusting attachment to the vacuum.

      a. Detailed attention should be given to moldings, corners, and baseboards.

      b. Cobwebs are greasy and should be lifted with an upward stroke.

  2. Walls, ceiling, and woodwork which are soiled should be well cleaned.

      a. If the paint is washable, proceed as you did in the kitchen. (A wall painted in flat paint cleans better if the excess dirt is removed with wall-paper dough before it is washed.)

  3. To wash walls papered in washable paper, first test the paper in an inconspicuous spot.

      a. Clean with gentle strokes using a solution of cold water and mild detergent and a fine, well-wrung sponge.

  4. Non-washable paper and paint can be cleaned with wallpaper cleaner.

      a. Gently rub the surface, using overlapping strokes to prevent streaking.

F. Radiators and hot-air outlets should be cleaned.

  1. The vacuum cleaner attachment or a long-handled duster or damp sponge will do the job here.

G. Mirrors and picture glass should be carefully cleaned with either commercial or homemade glass cleaner.

H. Wooden picture frames may be cleaned with furniture polish.

I. Gilded frames should be cleaned with dry-cleaning fluid.

J. Leather book bindings and leather upholstered furniture can be protected from drying by rubbing in leather conditioner or saddle soap.

K Windows should be the next project.

L. Venetian blinds should be cleaned according to their soilage.

    1. Use the vacuum cleaner dusting brush.

    2. Use an especially made Venetian blind cleaner or place an old sock or glove over your hand, dip it in a detergent solution and wash each blind slat.

    3. Suds blinds in the bathtub.

        a. Protect them with a clean-up wax.

M. Window shades are next on the agenda.

    1. Washable window shades should be first dusted and then lightly cleaned with a sponge and soapsuds, rinsed and wiped dry.

    2. Non-washable shades may be cleaned with an art gum eraser or wallpaper cleaner.

N. Bare floors should be cleaned while the furniture is away from the walls.

    1. Dust with a dry dust mop.

    2. Apply a paste or solvent-base wax.

    3. Polish wax to a lustre.

O. Upholstered furniture.

    1. Clean with vacuum.

    2. Clean with upholstery shampoo. (Avoid cleaning too frequently because shampoos tend to dull and fade fabric.)

P. Slipcovers

    1. Wash according to type of fabric.

        a. Most of them can be done in an automatic washer and dryer.

            1. Treat an excessively soiled area by applying a paste or liquid detergent and letting it soak ten minutes.

        b. To avoid ironing the entire slipcover, remove from the line or dryer while it is still slightly damp, press the pleats and ruffles and then place it on the furniture, and it will dry wrinkle free.

Q. Lampshades
   1. Clean with a special lampshade brush or the vacuum
      cleaner brush.
   2. Washable fabric lampshades, provided they are
      stitched together and not glued, can be shampooed
      in the bathtub with mild suds and thoroughly rinsed
      with a damp sponge.
R. Wipe off light bulbs, and thoroughly wash, rinse, and
   dry the light-diffusing bowls.
S. Dust and polish the lamp bases.
T. Tables—with a little special attention can look almost as
   good as new.
   1. Remove old wax by using a mild soap suds and
      well-wrung cloth. Rinse well.
   2. Conceal scratches, using either commercial or home-
      made products.
   3. Polish.
U. Rug—rates the final cleaning job.
   1. Regular and thorough vacuuming is the best way to
      keep up a carpet. Spots which appear should be
      removed by using either commercial or homemade
      spot removers. Be certain after spotting to blot the
      area thoroughly with absorbent tissue paper to
      remove the stain and to dry the area thoroughly.
   2. Clean (shampoo) your carpet only when it is
      absolutely necessary. The frequency of cleaning is
      determined by the carpet fibre and traffic in the
      home.
      a. Generally speaking, you are money ahead in the
         long run to have a carpet professionally cleaned
         by a reliable cleaning service.
      b. If circumstances are such that you must shampoo
         your carpet yourself, rug shampooers, both elec-

tric and non-electric are available. Care should be given so that the carpet doesn't become too wet in this process.

III BEDROOMS

A. Closets—devote an entire day to them.
1. Remove contents.
2. Hang clothing on the line to air.
3. Toss plastic garment bags and shoulder covers into the washer, unzipped and without hangers, and then dry them at low heat. By adding two heavy bath towels to the wash along with the plastic bags, the static will be decreased, and the bags will be cleaned better.
4. Vacuum or wash interior of the closet.
5. Spray with moth insecticide and mildew spray if you live in a damp climate.
6. Replace contents in a systematic way.
B. Dresser drawers.
1. Remove and sort the contents.
2. Vacuum each drawer thoroughly as well as the inside of the chest.
3. Line the drawers with fresh paper, if needed.
4. Replace the contents.
C. Continue to clean as you did in the living room. This time include dressing table skirts and valances.
D. Use appropriate vacuum cleaner attachments to clean the mattress and box springs, and then use a mattress-freshener spray to do away with musty odors.
E. Wash mattress pads and other bedding.
F. Dust and polish the furniture.
G. Wash scatter rugs.

1. Spray them with a nonskid solution or sew rubber canning jar rings on the reverse side.
H. Clean and polish the floor.
I. Shampoo the carpet.

IV BATHROOM– last on our list so that it could serve as a supply center while rest of house was being cleaned.
A. Remove contents from medicine cabinet and other closets.
1. Take a complete inventory of the medicines and other supplies and throw away old prescriptions, unlabeled bottles, and any other supplies which are no longer of value.
2. Clean the interior of the cabinets.
3. Dry thoroughly and replace contents.
B. Toss shower curtain, curtains, rugs, and mats in the washer.
1. Plastic bath items can be washed automatically in delicate fabric cycle as were your garment bags. (See III A.) If water marks on them are bad, use a water softener instead of a detergent. A vinegar rinse may also help.
C. Wash walls, shower stall, and tile.
1. For a water-stained shower stall, spray the walls with glass cleaner or wipe them with a sponge dipped in an ammonia solution and then wipe dry with a piece of turkish toweling.
D. Clean tub, basin, and toilet bowl.
E. Clean and clear the drains with a drain cleaner.
F. Mop and wax the floor.
G. Complete your cleaning by hanging fresh curtains.

Now, after all your hard work, be certain to KEEP your home lovely and clean. A neighbor once commented, "I used to think that you cleaned house and then let it go until it became so dirty you couldn't stand it any longer, and then you cleaned again." She added, "But now I've learned the secret to KEEPING a home clean by following a systematic plan of daily picking up, frequent sweeping and dusting, and then a thorough weekly cleaning." My neighbor further commented that changing her philosophy of "cleaning house when you have to" to "keeping my home neat and clean" transfomed her attitude toward housework from "a thing of drudgery" to "a very satisfying experience," and that it also changed her reputation of being a poor housekeeper to that of keeper of a lovely home.

By systematically keeping your home clean through daily and weekly work, coupled with extra deep cleaning periodically, you will be able to rejoice in your sparkling home all year round, realizing that "cleanliness is next to godliness." Rumford said, "So great is the effect of cleanliness upon man that it extends even to his moral character. Virtue never dwelt long with filth; nor do I believe there ever was a person scrupulously attentive to cleanliness, who was a consummate villain."

FACET NO. 10
INCENTIVE PLAN

An ideal homemaker's activities are well-balanced. Though she may be noted for a speciality and devote a major part of her time to one particular phase, she doesn't spend all of her time cooking, or does she concentrate just on sewing, or on cleaning, or on reading, or on outside interests. She reaches out to include in her life stimulating projects which serve as an incentive to her.

You recall that we quoted the poet, Robert Frost, as saying, "Learn to do the things you HAVE to do more quickly and effortlessly—save minutes—and you will gain an extra hour or more every day to do the things you really WANT to do. . . ."

The things that you really want to do—the special projects listed in your appointment book—serve as incentives to buzz through routine jobs and help focus your mind beyond the duty at hand. (These projects are also good cures for feeling bored or isolated.)

I find it terribly frustrating to try to work on a special project while the house is disorderly or dishes are stacked in the sink, but I find that by looking forward to working on a special project after the routine work is finished, I enjoy the work more and get it done much faster. Then the special project is like the dessert after a nourishing meal.

Think for a minute about some of the special projects you would like to include in your "Incentive Plan." For me, these projects would include, among others: creative activities with our children; keeping up baby books and scrapbooks; working

on my files; letter writing; reading; sewing; preparing holiday decorations for our home; entertaining; and helping others.

Just as special projects serve as incentives to get work done, so do outside activities offer an incentive. Not only are they very enjoyable to you as a homemaker, but they are beneficial to you as well.

The story is told of a woman who was taken by her husband to see a psychiatrist. After analyzing her thoroughly, the psychiatrist reported that her mind was confused. The husband replied, "I just don't see how her mind can be confused. She hasn't been out of the kitchen for three years."

Activities and positions of responsibility in the church, community, PTA, or other service organizations help to balance our lives and serve to inspire us and increase our enthusiasm. As you return home from a particular assignment or meeting, you do so with lifted spirits, greater goals, and loftier ideals. Also, having to be prepared to do a specific thing at a certain time is an excellent force in aiding a time budget! I find that church work, in moderation, actually helps me to have more time, instead of less, for my homemaking responsibilities.

Other types of activities such as luncheons and showers are fine forms of relaxation and entertainment and offer a stimulating exchange of ideas among other women.

Adult education clases are educational as well as enjoyable. Sports of various types are beneficial.

Evenings out with your husband enjoying dinners (with someone else doing the cooking and dishwashing), shows, concerts, theatrical productions, or get-togethers in the homes of other couples are an excellent break in your demanding life as a homemaker and bring about fine companionship with your husband.

Don't hesitate about leaving your children with a reliable baby sitter from time to time. This helps prevent children

from being mommy's babies and causes Mother and Daddy to "love them more than ever" when they return.

There is just one word of caution, however. These activities are advantageous only when they are held within moderation. If they are overdone and carried to the extreme, they become too common and no longer offer diversion, and their purpose is defeated.

During your child-raising years, certainly caring for, training, and playing with your children is your number one project. But still, through good management, there is a little time for you to pursue some personal interest in the adult world for your satisfaction and development. All too often young mothers remark, "Oh, I'll do that when my children are raised," only to discover, much to their dismay, that by that time they are too far out of practice to do very much. Even during the time our children demand such a great deal from us, it is essential to prevent our minds, hands, and personalities from becoming rusty by following some stimulating incentive plans. This not only provides a happier, more effective motherhood for you, but it also prepares the way for a useful, rewarding grandmotherhood.

This Incentive Plan is a sure way to keep you from feeling bored, or from feeling that life is all drudgery. It will do wonders to help you feel satisfied and creative about your homemaking and will add increased meaning to your life.

You can't do everything at once, but you can do some thing at once!

FACET NO. 11

FROM A HOUSE TO A HOME

*An ideal homemaker is able to transform four
walls into a home by creating both spiritual
and physical beauty therein.*

Every house has a personality—you can feel it as you enter
the door. Just as people differ in their personalities, so do
homes. Some homes are gay and interesting, others are more
sedate, while still others are quite plain. Some are houses;
others are homes.

Have you ever stopped to consider that the personality of
a home is usually a reflection of the personalities that dwell in
it. Winston Churchill said, "We shape our houses then our
houses shape us." Because your home will REFLECT your
personality and because it will also AFFECT your personality,
it's well worth putting forth special effort to have it just as
you would like. Your home is undoubtedly the most important
temporal possession in your life. Unless you do something to
create in it both spiritual and physical beauty, it remains
nothing more than a shelter. A sunny, gracious atmosphere in
your home makes you feel radiant and happy. Dull surroundings push you into a depression. Plan to do something each
day to improve your home so that your improvement will
never cease. Then it can bring out the best that is in you and
the others who dwell therein. Make your home a haven of
peace and beauty for your family. Make it a place where
friends will want to visit again.

One striking observation we made while in Holland is that
the homes in that tiny land have choice personalities. The
window sills in those red brick homes with the red tiled roofs

are always filled with rows of flower pots—usually containing geraniums. The windows are large—with never a blind or a screen to cover them. These glistening windows add to the sparkle of the home's personality. Many of the homes are named. Above a door you might see names such as: Sunny Corner, Sunbeam, Sun Cottage, Peace Haven, Tranquility, or Peaceful Nook. The names symbolize the dreams and desires of the Dutch people; they reflect what is in their hearts. Warmth and sunshine and pleasantness, together with peace and tranquility and contentment! THESE ARE THE THINGS WHICH MAKE A HOUSE A HOME!

After establishing order and cleanliness in your home, it is fun, as well as worthwhile, to add the special touches which will give your home increased interest and personality. Here are some decorating hints to guide you to do so.

I   GENERAL DECORATING HINTS.

    A. "Good taste has no price tag."

    B. The best criterion of a well-decorated room is that it serves its purpose and is pleasing in appearance, not just that it follows rigid rules. Rooms should be able to be lived in and should also be a source of pride to the residents.

    C. A house should achieve four main objectives:

        1. It should be functional—fitting the needs of the family and containing a place for everyone and everything.

        2. It should be economical—not necessarily cheap, but the best for your money. Remember, cost isn't only the initial expense; consider durability and maintenance.

        3. It should be individual—expressing you and your family.

4. It should be beautiful—representing good taste in form, line, light, color, texture, and space.

D. Each item in the house should fulfill its function.

E. There should be unification of a theme. For instance, you should have a good transition of color from one room to the next; furniture and accessories should be compatible in style.

F. The accessories should lend enrichment.

G. Each room should have a comfortable feeling of balance.

H. There should be a center of interest in each room such as the fireplace, a table, or headboard on a bed, and also lesser subordinate interests.

I. Each room should have a gentle sense of rhythm.

II COLOR—should be one of the most influential factors in the home.

A. Monochromatic: made of one hue or color, lightened and darkened.

1. This must be varied with different kinds of textures.

2. Sharp blacks and whites can be used as accents (in pillows, for instance) to make the other color sparkle.

3. If not handled carefully, this color scheme can be monotonous.

4. It can, however, be smart, charming, and restful.

MONOCHROMATIC

B. Analogous: made with colors which are adjacent on a color wheel. (For example, the yellows, oranges, and greens, or the reds, blues, and violets.)

   1. Usually three to six colors are used.

   2. This scheme is generally very popular in modern interiors.

ANALOGOUS

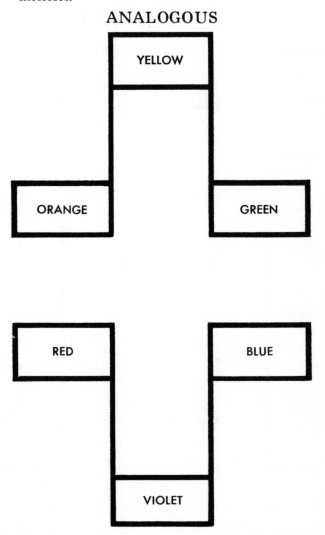

C. Complementary: several kinds are possible.
   1. Direct Complementary: made by using two colors that are opposite each other on the color wheel. (For example, orange and blue, red and green, yellow and violet.)

DIRECT COMPLEMENTARY

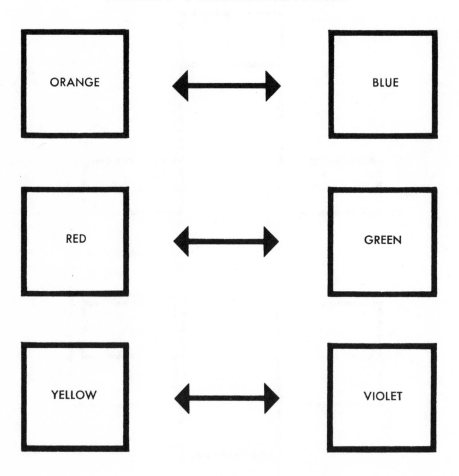

2. Split Complementary: made by choosing one color and then adding the two colors on either side of its complement. (For example: yellow may be the first choice. Its direct complement is purple. On one side of purple is blue-violet; on the other side is red-violet. Thus yellow, blue-violet, and red-violet can be used.)

SPLIT COMPLEMENTARY

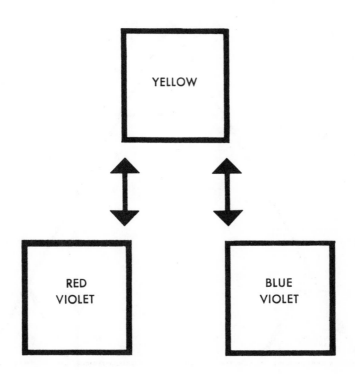

3. Triad Complementary: made by placing a triangle (real or imaginary) on a color wheel and using the three colors that come at the three points. (For example: red, yellow, and blue, or orange, green, and purple.) This color scheme is generally very bright and gay and can be used well in playrooms.

TRIAD COMPLEMENTARY

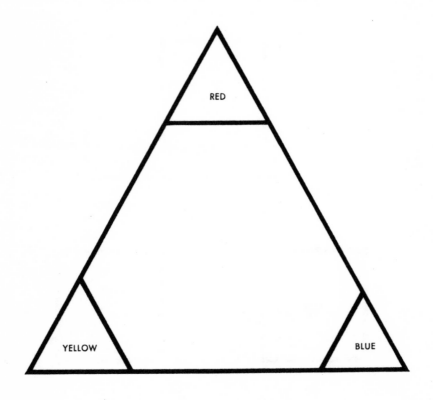

4. Alternate Complementary: made by taking a pair of direct complements, such as blue and orange, choosing one color from each side of them. (For example: on either side of blue is blue-green and blue-violet. On either side of orange is red and yellow.)

ALTERNATE COMPLEMENTARY

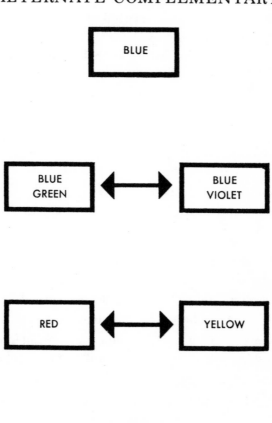

5. Double Complementary: made by using two pairs of complements. (For example: shades of yellow and violet (purple) with shades of blue and orange.) A recent trend is to have a multi-colored room. In order to achieve beauty in such a room, the decorating needs to be done carefully and well. There are three ways to plan such a room: (See diagram on page 131.)

    a. Start with a neutral background, such as an off-white, sandy beige, dove gray, sage brush, or grayed pink or blue. Select three or four colors you like together and play these against the background. (For example: these colors may be predominant in a picture you like.)

    b. Start with a multi-color background, such as print wallpaper or drapes, and then repeat three to five of the colors.

    c. Start with two or three contrasting colors of the same color family and then accent them.

III PRINCIPLES OF COLOR DECORATING.

  A. Never use equal proportions of warm and cool colors. (Warm colors are the yellows, pinks, reds, and oranges.) (Cool colors are the blues, greens, lavenders, and grays.)

  B. It is good to have one predominating color in a room.

  C. An easy formula to remember is: "Something dark and something light. Something dull and something bright."

  D. There are no "do's" and "don'ts" to color. The "HOW" is what is important.

IV PLANNING A COLOR SCHEME.

  A. Choose the color for the largest area first, such as the walls and ceiling. (If you want the ceiling to appear the

DOUBLE COMPLEMENTARY

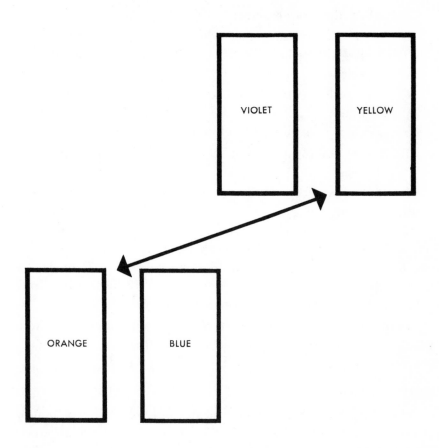

same color as the walls, paint it several shades lighter than the walls.)

    1. Backgrounds are generally best if subtle in color.

B. Select the floor-covering.

    1. A wall-to-wall carpet will tend to make a room look larger; smaller area rugs will make the room seem smaller.

C. Choose the colors and textures for the larger pieces of furniture, remembering to select an upholstery color which will harmonize with the wood.

D. Select colors for small chairs, accent pieces, pictures, and vases.

In the proximity of many universities in the nation are student housing villages where many young couples, living in what might be termed "glorified chicken coops" and operating on a shoestring, financially speaking, have made those tiny quarters look like a page from *Better Homes and Gardens.* (It is said that those student villages are the only place where one can hear four toilets flushing simultaneously!)

Here are some creative ideas gleaned from several of those villages. Perhaps you can use a few of them in your home, coupled with the good decorating hints just listed.

LIVING ROOM

An attractive sofa can be made out of either a hollow door or two large pieces of ¾" plywood screwed together. Then this can be stained or painted (Lamp Black with a white top is effective) and placed on either wooden or wrought iron legs. (These can be purchased in hardware departments.) Foam rubber, covered with a good fabric in your favorite color, is ideal for a cushion. However, for less expense, an old army cot mattress purchased in any army surplus store and attractively covered can serve just fine. Then complete the sofa by adding gaily colored toss pillows for the back.

One couple bought a nicely stuffed sofa for $5.00 from an ad in the paper. With $12.00 worth of good fabric, buttons, and thread (they used the webbing and cording from original sofa) they recovered the sofa, and it is lovely.

A TV stand can be made out of two sturdy suitcases which are just high enough. Make a square top and then sew a four-sided valance on it. (The valance can be made of same material as draperies.)

A coffee or cocktail table can be made from a hollow door (ash wood has an especially pretty grain). Cut the door down to the size you desire and glue the end strip back on. (An imperfect door can be purchased, placing the imperfect side down.) Place the door on either wooden or wrought iron legs and paint or stain it. One impressive finish is to paint the entire table with "Lamp Black" and then wipe this paint off the top. It becomes a lovely gray color, high-lighted by the wood grains. Sand it well, then go over it with a plastic glaze. Repeat the sanding and glazing process several times, and you'll have a table that could complement the finest of rooms.

Colored bed sheets can be used for draperies.

To enhance the walls, cut pictures from calendars or magazines and place in dime store frames.

Book shelves can be made from inexpensive pine boards, covered with burlap (using Blue Bird glue) and then wiping the burlap immediately with a damp cloth. The shelves are supported by rustic sand colored bricks, which match the burlap. (Cinder blocks or glass bricks can also be attractively used in this manner.)

Partitions between the living room and kitchen can be attractively made from inexpensive lattice work, decorated with planters and knickknacks. Another type of partition is made from white plastic clothes line rope (which can be purchased for a few cents a yard) interwoven in an interesting manner. Plywood can also be made into a decorative partition.

Inexpensive rugs and linoleum carpets provide attractive and new floor coverings.

KITCHEN

Gaily colored curtains, made from inexpensive fabrics or remnant items, add just the right touch.

If cupboards go only part way to the ceiling and if the space above them is needed for storage, a curtain along there adds color and keeps the items out of sight.

Bright appliance covers and hot pads in matching colors add to the charm of the kitchen.

Good-looking table and chair sets can be made from old ones found in second-hand stores. Chrome chairs repolished and the seats recovered with plastic fabric can look as good as new.

A particularly clever kitchen set can be made from wire stools—the type once used in ice cream parlors and obtained through second-hand stores—painted black with colorful corduroy cushions. A matching table complements the set.

Self-laid linoleum or tile can do a lot for an old wooden floor.

Decals on cupboards or canisters further brighten a room.

Closet and cupboard doors can be made from masonite or plywood painted to match the color scheme, or from fabrics or from old window shutters.

A handy pegboard for cooking utensils or pots and pans can be a real space maker.

Vinyl or terry cloth table cloths are work-savers and can be purchased in colors to match your color scheme. They're inexpensive and always clean!

Bamboo-type curtains are attractive and easy to care for and clean.

Additional cupboard space can be made from inexpensive boards bought from a lumber yard or by stacking apple boxes (ten cents at the grocer's) and decorating them.

BEDROOM

Construct a bed by placing a mattress on a plain bedstead and making your own attractive headboard from plastic material, a quilted fabric, or adhesive paper.

Chest of drawers can be unfinished furniture which you've painted or stained.

Apple boxes can also add to the cupboard space. If you'd like a change from painting and staining, try covering them with adhesive paper.

BATHROOM

A set of towels or terry cloth makes an attractive, absorbent, and shadow-proof bathroom curtain.

Suggestions for other furnishings and clever, but economical, accent pieces and holiday decorations can be found in magazines or in homes you visit. You can also get practical ideas by attending handicraft classes or Relief Society work meetings. Perhaps you can think up some clever tricks and ideas yourself! Besides having these creative touches add so much to a house, working on them can bring you a great deal of fun and satisfaction.

Don't forget to let flowers and plants, either artificial or real, add a special touch to your home. Tantalizing odors from freshly baked bread, cinnamon rolls, gingerbread, or beef stew as they permeate your home's atmosphere lend to its hominess and enchantment.

In summary, have pride in your home, be interested in it, be creative and imaginative, and it will reflect the best that is in you and change from a house to a home.

FACET NO. 12

GROW YOUR OWN—
OR CHILDREN CAN HELP

She will be ideal in her role as a homemaker, not only because of the countless current values, but because her example and teachings will live at least another generation through her children. She must help them to be valuable diamonds, too.

No matter how efficient or organized you might be, you'll have an almost impossible job keeping your home in order and the housework caught up *unless* you have the cooperation and help of your children. I don't believe any woman can work hard an; fast enough to keep things cleaned up and picked up after several careless, thoughtless children.

On the other hand, when children work with you rather than against you, the housework isn't much of a problem at all. And as a result, there's time for lots of family fun. In fact, the best families I know all work together and then play and grow together.

And besides your needing your children's help, the children need the training which comes through having responsibility and learning to work. Your home is the training ground for your children's life. I believe that children who are required to do a few basic chores every day to the best of their ability learn how to be good, thorough workers, and they learn how to apply themselves and use their time well.

Through consistently performing daily tasks such as making a bed and leaving a room in order, children develop habits which will serve them well for life. I'm sure there's not a woman in town who doesn't know how to make a bed, do a batch of dishes or keep a room orderly. But not all of these women know how to make themselves do these things every single day. That's the challenge. So during the years when your children are young and their habits are so easily formed, help them to learn some consistency, routine, and self discipline. They'll benefit from the dividends for the rest of their lives.

I'd like to illustrate this philosophy by telling you about a young eleven-year-old friend of ours who lived in a rural area. His parents had just purchased a new cow and we asked this boy who milked the cow. "Well," he said, "it's like this. I milk the cow in the morning to save me, and Dad milks the cow at night to save the cow."

Now, I'm sure you agree that it's important for both you and the children that they have some responsibilities about the home and yard. You realize that over the years you should do less and less *for* your children so you can do more and more *with* them. But the big question is: HOW CAN YOU ENGAGE THE HELP OF YOUR CHILDREN WITHOUT BEING AT WAR WITH THEM?

Well, this is what I want to talk to you about. And let's do so under five main categories.

First: LET YOUR CHILDREN KNOW WHAT IS EX-PECTED OF THEM AND BE CONSISTENT IN YOUR REQUIREMENTS.

Think how confusing life would be for you if you didn't have guidelines like the Ten Commandments! Or imagine being hired for a job and then having no one tell you or show you what you were supposed to do!

So, give your children the advantage of telling them exactly what you expect. You'll find this in itself does a great deal to merit their cooperation.

For example, in our home before the children eat breakfast they must dress, (It seems that it takes a child about two

minutes to dress *before* breakfast and about two hours to dress afterwards!), hang up their night clothes, make their beds, wash their faces and hands, brush their teeth and comb their hair. Then after breakfast, before they can leave for school or play they must do other chores such as helping clear the kitchen, dusting, cleaning the bathroom, emptying the garbage, feeding the cat, practicing the piano. And before story time each evening they must pick up their play things and put away their clothes. Now, of course, the duties and responsibility will vary as the children grow, but the principle or the organization remains the same.

Along this same line, it's important that you be consistent in requiring a child's help every day. Now, the jobs may vary from day to day, but a child should get used to helping every day in some way. If you have your children help you yesterday but not today, and then you should ask them to help you tomorrow, it's likely that they'll try to argue with you and talk you out of it because they know you're inconsistent and a pushover.

So decide what you expect from your children and then stick to it. BE CONSISTENT. Your children will soon accept their assignments as a matter of routine and the discussions and arguments will cease.

The second category is: MAKE WORK EASY FOR THEM.

Remember, children are novices at housework. Don't expect them to be as clever as you are after many years of experience.

Speaking of experience, an employer, interviewing an applicant, remarked' "You certainly ask high wages for a man with no experience." "Well," came the answer, "that's because it's so much harder work when you don't know anything about what you're doing."

And don't just tell your children to do a task. Show them

and teach them how by working with them. For instance, have
your children help make their beds—that is, they work on one
side of the bed while you work on the other—from the time
they're big enough to walk until they're four or five years old.
Then by that time they really know how to make a bed
properly, and their arms and legs are long enough so it's
possible for them to do a good job. And then their efforts are
a source of pride to them as well as to you. A few minutes
of your time for several mornings can teach a child how to do
a good job of cleaning the bathroom or cleaning up the
kitchen.

It's most helpful to give your children low shelves and low
clothes rods so that they're within their reach. The little
containers I mentioned for toys (remember, the toy bags?),
well, these make it easier and more fun to care for the toys.

You might make a little sample table place setting out of
colored paper for your children to copy from as they set the
table. They'll find it fun to try to make each place setting
look like the sample. You'll find this idea illustrated below.

Now, the third category: USE EFFECTIVE DISCIPLINARY MEASURES WHEN NECESSARY.

Once in a while more drastic measures must be taken to get children to work. The experts say that "Wise parents understand that discipline should be a *learning* experience and not just a *punishment*. Through punishment a parent controls a child's action. But that's only part of the task. Through good discipline a parent can teach a child to control his own actions.

"Life itself should be the greatest teacher and can suggest the best methods of discipline, if we will just let it. For instance, if we as parents will let a child experience the consequence of his own acts, then he has a true learning situation."

Here are some examples to illustrate the point. If a child's basic morning chores have not been completed, then he can't leave for play or school until they've been done.

One morning, a mother failed to check her boy's room before he left for school, and after he'd gone, she discovered that he hadn't made his bed. So she went to the school and asked the teacher if she could take him home for a few minutes because there was something he hadn't done. The teacher was wise enough to cooperate. The boy went home with her, made his bed, and returned to school. Needless to say, he hasn't failed to make his bed since. (And by the way, this teacher uses the same technique. No student can go out for recess or leave for home until his assignments have been completed. As a result, she has a room full of outstanding students who have lots of respect for her as a teacher.)

You'll find that these consequences really teach children the lessons of life quickly, and they eliminate much scolding and nagging on the part of parents. Consequently rebellion and resentment are not built up within the child. A child has a keen sense of fair play, and when the "punishment fits the crime" as in the case of a consequence, he takes his medicine and seldom needs a second dose.

If a child's dirty clothes are not put in the hamper, then the clothes can't be washed by mother. He either wears dirty clothes or washes them himself.

If he doesn't put away his toys they may be placed on the "unwanted toy shelf" until he has missed them sufficiently to take better care of them.

If older children leave articles of clothing and other belongings littered around, these articles may be placed in the "Mad Bag." The mad bag is just a large grocery bag in which neglected items are kept until redeemed by the owner with a nickel or dime. The money, of course, goes to the person who had to pick up the items to compensate him for the undue "maid" service he or she had to render. Or if the owner of the neglected items is low on cash, he may redeem his things by performing some special service for the person who had to pick up after him.

When children balk about doing the dishes, the consequence is that anyone who is "too tired" or "too busy" to do the dishes, is also "too tired" or "too busy" to receive any phone calls or watch television that evening and must spend his time in his room.

A young boy was making it a habit of leaving his bike out in the yard every evening instead of putting it in the garage. This was brought to an abrupt halt when his father got him out of bed one night to put his bicycle away.

In one home where the children's wraps and belongings were always tossed and scattered over the railing of the stairway instead of being placed in the cloak closet, the mother solved the problem by putting up a sign which read: FIVE CENTS A THROW.

I know of a mother who was getting more than her share of exercise cleaning up the spills under the toddler's chair at the dinner table. It was almost like a game for the child to watch his mother crawling in and around the chair and table legs cleaning up the messes. Then one day the mother got smart and had the child clean up the messes. There wasn't much more spilling after that, as you can guess.

So, let life's consequences teach your children the things they need to know. That's good discipline as far as helping children do their chores is concerned. And after a little of that, you'll be ready for lots of the positive approach.

And that brings me to the fourth point which is:

ENCOURAGE YOUR CHILDREN IN THEIR EFFORTS—LET
THEM KNOW OF YOUR APPRECIATION.

It's been often said that "a pat on the back goes a lot
farther than a kick in the you-know-what." And this is
expecially true with children. Children wither under criticism
and they blossom under encouragement and appreciation. Even
if it's necessary to correct their habits in some way, remember:
"A barber always lathers his customers before he shaves them."

So first point out the good things in your children's work
and then in a constructive way, rather than in a critical way,
suggest methods for improvement. For instance, you might say,
"Billy, I'm really pleased with the way you make your bed
every morning without having to be reminded. That show's
you're really growing up! I'm sure you're ready now for me to
show you how to put the bedspread just a bit straighter so
your bed will look really sharp."

Now, along with encouraging your children and expressing
appreciation in the usual ways, it can be lots of fun for
everyone concerned to do some things a little different. Have
any of your children ever found a special thank-you note from
you tucked under their pillows? Have you ever included a
thank-you note for some special service on your son's part in
his lunch along with the sandwiches and an apple? Or how
about a little expression of thanks in verse taped to your
daughter's mirror? Here's a sample ditty:

> I'm really not a poet,
> But in some way I must show it—
> That I think it's really great
> The way you keep your room so straight!

So be sure to encourage your children and show your
appreciation. Children love to help with the work in such an
atmosphere.

I'm sure you've heard the old story about the farmer who

couldn't get his stubborn mule to move. First, he tried to build a fire under the animal. Well, the mule did get up and move away from the heat, but he sat down again as soon as things were cool. Then he tried to get him going by beating him. As you can imagine, this was terribly hard on both the mule as well as the farmer. Finally, the farmer tied a bunch of carrots to the end of a stick, dangled the carrots over the mule's nose and the mule trotted down the road.

Some children are just a little like mules. And, therefore, the best way to get them going is to dangle some carrots in front of them. In other words, give them an incentive.

That's the fifth category: GIVE YOUR CHILDREN AN INCENTIVE, or make work fun for them. So now I'd like to toss out some "carrots," so to speak, to you. Maybe some of these will help you motivate your children. There's one problem, though. I'm afraid you'll have to provide a different carrot for each child! And even worse, you might have to have a different carrot every day for each child. So start collecting these carrots if you haven't done so already. You never know when you'll be able to find just the right one to get a child into action.

We all work better with incentives. So give your children lots of them until they're mature enough to have their own incentives and know the value of work and accomplishment.

So here we go with the "carrots." The other day I heard a father say to his young boys, "When those weeds are pulled, we'll go swimming." And then a young mother say, "When we've tidied up the kitchen, we'll go to the park for a swing."

Another father plays army with his three little sons. They begin to march and drill and before the boys realize what's happened, they've picked up their toys and paraded off to bed. And the amazing thing about this is that this fun, positive approach takes lots less time and is certainly better for everyone involved than the usual going-to-bed struggle.

I know some little girls who help best when declared "Little Homemakers" and are given an apron and a "schedule." Of course, this "schedule" is nothing but a list of two or three simple duties. But it really works!

Children like to wear a little hand puppet (maybe one made from a stocking or paper bag) and then have the puppet pick up the toys and clothing. Or, the children themselves could pretend to be the puppets and mother could "pull the strings."

Or the game "Twenty-Pick-Up" is a really workable one. Say, the playroom is cluttered with toys and scraps of paper. Call the children together and ask them all to pick up twenty things—or whatever number of items seems necessary. Everything disappears like magic because this way the children see both the beginning and the end of their chores, and they don't have to worry whether or not others in the family are doing their part, too. So try "Twenty-Pick-Up" the next time a room or the yard is cluttered or when someone drops the can of marbles.

Children like to have charts with their duties listed on them. A gold star at the end of the week if all the work is done is often just the incentive children need.

Many families enjoy the "Job Jar" idea. All you need is an ordinary glass bottle—or any other container for that matter—filled with slips of paper on which various jobs and duties are written. Then every child draws five or six slips to see what his jobs for the following week will be.

One time a mother asked her little boy who wasn't paying any attention to her if he was hard of hearing. "Oh, no," he said, "I'm just hard of listening." You know, this can happen. Sometimes our children hear our voices so much that they become mother-deaf and tune out. So if you've done enough talking lately, try note writing for a change. Here's a little verse one mother taped to the doorway of her daughter's room:

> Great scott! don't be a fool;
> Get your bed made
> Before you go to school!

I'm sure there are as many more "carrots" as there is imagination. So think them up yourself. Be sure to have several to choose from whenever the occasion demands. Try the incentive plan on your children.

There's one more idea which sort of wraps up all the others I've been talking about. In fact, this could be the most consistently effective thing in organizing a family team for the greatest amount of productivity with the least amount of reminding. It's called a "Chore Box." You'll find a drawing of this on page 148 to help you visualize what I'm talking about. As you can see, there's a little slot for job cards for each child in the family. Mom, you and Dad can have a slot, too, if you'd like. Of course, the object is to get the cards moved from the "jobs to do" rack up to the "jobs finished" rack. I think you'll find that your children really like this idea because it helps outline and organize work; it shows a starting and stopping point with regard to chores; and it eliminates a lot of irritating reminding and nagging on mother's part.

Mothers are enthusiastic about this Chore Box because it helps them to be consistent in having the children help every day. It helps them arrange chores according to the day of the week and rotates them from child to child so there's variety and learning for all. It helps them keep track of lots of odd jobs and who is responsible for them, and it helps them follow through to make sure the job is done and done right. By the way, if you find something wasn't done thoroughly and well, you can slip the card back to the bottom of the rack and your child will have to do it over again.

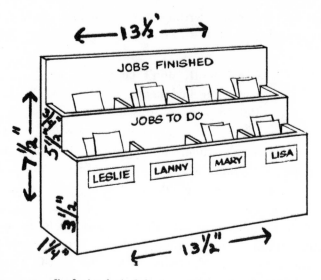

You may find it helpful to write the morning chores on yellow slips of paper; the noon chores on pink slips; and the evening chores on blue. In this way, the children are responsible for doing all the yellow slips before they leave for play or school. You don't want their beds made last thing at night just to get the slip of paper up in the next rack! You may even have a few white slips of paper for S.O.S. jobs. These are for the times when someone is ill, company is coming, you're preparing for a trip or some other situation calls for extra help.

It can be lots of fun to occasionally include a bonus card stating something like this' "Go to the store and buy an ice cream cone." (A coin would be taped to the card.) Or maybe the card would read: "Come to Mother for a special hug." Or, "Yes, you may go swimming today."

You'll find a list of suggested chores for children on pages 153 to 157.

A chore box can be made from plywood, masonite, naugahyde, vinyl cloth, heavy fabric, cereal boxes, or construction paper. It can be decorated to match the kitchen or be strictly a functional item. Either way, all you have to do is stuff it with jobs every night in preparation for a great experience in family teamwork.

In many homes children are not paid for doing any of their routine chores. These chores are part of living together as a family just like the meals and fun times. If you pay your child to make his bed and then the day comes when he has a job and earns plenty of money, he'll see no reason why he should continue making his bed. On the other hand, there should be a few paid jobs to supplement the children's allowance and to teach them the satisfaction of earning money. But these are not routine, basic chores. These paid jobs are chores for which you might hire someone to perform and hire instead your own child. For instance, you might hire your older girls to baby sit the younger children. You might hire your boy to paint the house when he is old enough. Now, if the girls don't want to baby sit or if your boy doesn't want to paint the house, you could hire someone else without losing face. It's a business proposition. Do you see the difference between a basic chore and a paid job?

Just a word about the various ages and stages of children and how they relate to their chores. Toddlers and very young children are eager to help. It's wise to capitalize on their willingness. It is inconsistent to refuse to let a child help set the table when he's two and then when he's six, demand that he set the table. At least the two-year-old can place napkins and silverware. Unless the job is either dangerous or destructive you should let a child have the fun and growth which comes from trying.

Then the novelty of helping—unless the task is especially challenging—begins to wane as the child approaches three. A pre-schooler must be motivated before he will work. Lots of the suggestions already mentioned in this chapter appeal to children of this age group.

I believe that children from age six to eleven usually give the best help around the house. So this is the age to train them to really be effective in their responsibilities and to make certain that proper work habits and traits are being formed. Also, this is the best age for using the chore box. You can draw pictures to represent chores for the younger children, but a chore box works best for school-age children.

As you may well know, many older children and teenagers are so very busy with studies, part-time jobs and social activities that they don't have as much time to help around the house as they did when they were younger. Even so, if a teenager had had *early* and *consistent* training in doing chores so that he has good work habits, and if the home is organized so that the time spent on chores is at a minimum, there are a number of things he can do to help. Even the busiest teenager should keep his own room and clothing in order and should not make work for someone else through his sloppiness and inconsideration.

Times have changed and there generally is not enough outside work or heavy chores to provide a boy with enough responsibility. So it's all right for a boy to do any type of work around the home. I do believe, however, that the heavier jobs should be his first responsibility. But good work habits, dependability, careful and wise use of time, and thoroughness can be learned whether through milking cows or doing the dishes.

As a boy carries out household chores, his mother may remind him occasionally that this is all helping him to someday be a good business executive or construction engineer or to succeed in any profession. Also, this will help him to be a more considerate, understanding and thoughtful husband. Just as long as a boy has a good father image—his father is the head of the house and is worthy of everyone's respect—and that he can see his mother as a gracious, lovely homemaker, household chores can only make him grow to be a better man.

If for some reason your children have been negligent about doing their chores or you haven't trained and taught them to work as you should, you might feel that now is the time to mend the situation. BE CAREFUL! It's inviting disaster to suddenly spring a new policy on the family. It's much wiser to set the stage for it. So wait until just the right moment, say during a pleasant family hour while you're enjoying rootbeer floats or some other favorite treat, and then explain your new plans. Help your children see that it's important for you to do less for them so you can do more with them. Then assign the chores a few at a time so your children won't feel over-whelmed. Two jobs done well are worth six on the list!

Teaching children to work and putting up with all their messes and inadequacies is a real challenge. It would be lots easier to shoo your children out of the house, lock the door, and do it all yourself. But that's not what mothers are for. When someone said that mothers are supposed to sacrifice for their children, I'm sure they had this in mind.

It takes years of teaching, training, showing, patience, diligence, understanding, and encouragement along with lots and lots of follow-up to really prepare a child to be a good worker who can make a contribution in life. But when he finally learns, his accomplishments and successes will make all your efforts more than worthwhile.

So remember the five categories for engaging the help of your children:

1.   LET YOUR CHILDREN KNOW WHAT IS EXPECTED OF THEM AND BE CONSISTENT IN YOUR REQUIREMENTS.

2.   MAKE WORK EASY FOR THEM.

3.   USE EFFECTIVE DISCIPLINARY MEASURES WHEN NECESSARY.

4.   ENCOURAGE   YOUR   CHILDREN   IN   THEIR EFFORTS—LET THEM KNOW OF YOUR APPRECIATION.

5.   GIVE YOUR CHILDREN AN INCENTIVE.

A wise man put all this philosophy in a nutshell when he said: "A few headaches now will save you from heartaches later on."

SUGGESTED CHORES FOR CHILDREN

"Home is the training ground for life."

"It is important to do *less for* your children so you can do *more with* them."

"Ideal families work together so they can then play and grow together."

Three-Year-Old Child

DAILY	WEEKLY	WHEN NECESSARY
Before Breakfast	Before Play	help clean closet and drawers
dress	empty waste baskets	
put pajamas away	tend garden (in	
brush teeth	season)	
wash face	clean up assigned	
comb hair	area of yard	
make bed (with help)		
tidy up bedroom		
Before Play		
dust bedroom furniture		
After Lunch		
clear lunch table, help load dish-washer		
nap		
Before Story Hour and Bedtime		
pick up toys, etc.		
prepare for bed		

Five-Year-Old Child

DAILY	WEEKLY	WHEN NECESSARY
Before Breakfast dress put pajamas away brush teeth wash face comb hair make bed (with help occasionally) tidy up room **Before Play** clear breakfast table load dishwasher and help clean up kitchen clean television screen dust bedroom furniture **Before Lunch** put playthings away set table **After Lunch** quiet time (reading, games, coloring, etc.) **Before Story Hour and Bedtime** pick up toys, etc. prepare for bed put away clothes brush teeth	**Before Play** empty waste baskets clean tile walls in bathroom tend garden (in season) clean up assigned area of yard	help clean closet and drawers

Six-Year-Old Child

DAILY	WEEKLY	WHEN NECESSARY

Before Breakfast
dress
put pajamas away
brush teeth
wash face
comb hair
make bed
tidy up room
feed fish and turtle

Before School or Play
dust bedroom furniture
set breakfast table
take out kitchen garbage

After Lunch
return to school or quiet time for reading, crafts, etc.

After Dinner
clear table, load dishwasher and help clean up kitchen (alternates with 8-year-old sister every other evening)

Before Story Hour and Bedtime
pick up toys, etc.
prepare for bed
read and study

Before School or Play
clean fish and turtle bowls
return empty garbage cans to garage (Tuesday)
tend garden (in season)
clean up assigned area of yard
clean interior of car
sweep porches and walks
clean kitchen table and chair legs

help clean closet and drawers

Eight-Year-Old Child

DAILY	WEEKLY	WHEN NECESSARY

Before Breakfast
  dress
  put pajamas away
  brush teeth
  wash face, comb hair
  make bed
  tidy up room
Before School or Play
  wash bathroom mirrors
  dust parents' bedroom, living room and family room (any room not already assigned to younger child)
After Lunch
  return to school or quiet time for reading, crafts, etc
After Dinner
  clear table, load dishwasher and help clean up kitchen (alternates with 6-year-old brother every other evening)
Before Story Hour and Bedtime
  do homework
  prepare for bed (brush teeth, curl hair, do nails, etc.) put away clothes, etc.
  read and study
	Before School or Play
	  clean fingerprints from backdoor, etc.
	  clean glass in storm doors
	  iron flat articles
	  tend garden (in season)
	  clean up assigned area of yard
		polish furniture
		clean out closets and drawers
		help fold clothes (summer time)

All of this work, on the part of the children, requires a great deal of teaching, training, and *follow-up* on the part of the mother. The mother determines to a great extent the type of work habits children develop. It is also important that children have good attitudes toward their chores. Unless a job is done happily, it doesn't count!

As children grow older, they can continue to do the basic chores as previously listed. Additional chores, such as the following ones, can be added according to circumstances:

change linen on bed

clean entire bathroom

be able to clean up kitchen alone, although for companionship's sake it's fun to work with someone else

assume full responsibility for the care of one room (Kitchen Katie, Parlor Maid, Bathroom Beth, etc.)

vacuum (not only carpeting but ledges and ridges when necessary)

iron more complicated articles

cook and bake

plan meals

do marketing

sew and mend (girls)

repair jobs (boys)

practice musical instruments and take other types of lessons

scrub and wax floors

assume full responsibility of managing home for a week or so

take complete charge of personal grooming

assume full responsibility of personal clothing (shopping, care, etc.)

defrost refrigerator

clean range

help with heavy spring cleaning
    woodwork
    windows
    closets and cupboards
    walls

paint

refinish furniture

wash car

yard work

FACET NO. 13
FAMILY TRADITIONS

An ideal homemaker will encourage family traditions to add color and depth to the great picture she is painting. Instead of her home being just a "short-order house," it will be a hallowed place where children learn life's great lessons, gain proper values, and build memories which will enrich their lives and help determine their destinies.

A young boy whose father was an army officer heard some of his parents' friends lamenting the fact that these people had never been able to settle down and have a home. The boy quickly spoke up, "Oh, we always have a home. It's just that we sometimes don't have a house to put it in."

His mother had the ability of putting the HEART in a home.

A wonderful way to put the heart in a home is to enjoy family traditions. Many families have traditions or customs which may appear a little ridiculous to an outsider, but if they are viewed as dearly loved patterns of family life, they become precious and richly meaningful. These traditions, repeated throughout the years, become the very essence of family life.

A tradition needn't be spectacular; it can be as down-to-earth as a family picnic, asking the blessing before the meal, playing ball with Daddy after dinner, or enjoying a treat from Grandmother's cookie jar.

A gentleman, Norman M. Lobsenz, reported in an article appearing in *Good Housekeeping:* "Not long ago I was invited to dinner to celebrate a friend's birthday. There were ten of us at the table. . . . We were expectantly awaiting the birthday cake when one of the youngsters stood up and said, 'Time to march, everybody!'

"As the family all laughingly pushed back their chairs and rose, the guests followed suit. We formed a line, everyone's right hand on the shoulder of the person ahead, and began to march gaily through the house. It was a big house, and it was several minutes before we got back to the dining room. When we sat down, my friend said to me, 'I hope you don't think we're crazy. It's an old family custom.'

" 'How did it start?' I asked.

" 'When the children were little, it was hard for them to sit still through a meal. One night we got the idea of having everybody parade through the house between the main course and the dessert, to give the kids a chance to let off steam. Of course, as they grew older the marching became unnecessary, but by then it had become a sort of family ritual. So we kept doing it on special occasions. It sounds silly, but—well, it makes us all feel closer.' "

A choice young mother says she and her children look forward all year to wintertime when they can dress up in snowsuits and have a glorious time building snowmen, making igloos, and sliding down snow hills of their own making. Actually, she realizes the value of playing with children—on their level—all year round. This helps her children to be creative—a talent sadly lacking in this generation; it forms a companionship between them and her which will help weather the tensions and temptations of adolescence; and it enriches their childhood with memory-making fun.

Perhaps your family enjoys such traditions as playing car games as you travel, displaying the flag each national holiday, popping pop corn and eating it together, freezing your own ice cream and having the first spoonfull right from the dasher, camping or picnicking in the canyons, or visiting an amusement park each summer.

On a clear summer night it is a grand experience for a child to sleep outside under the stars. It's wonderful if children live on farms—or can visit them—and enjoy the seasonal events which take place. What excitement always accompanies harvest time when all the big, strong men come to help, and Mother and all the neighbor ladies prepare such unforgettable meals— sometimes with three choices of meats and desserts!

A very simple, yet significant tradition, is to read bedtime stories to your children. What a perfect opportunity to teach them and develop within them a love of reading and a love of good books.

Some of our best times are found in cooking or baking together.

A far-reaching tradition is to go with your family to church each Sunday. (To expedite getting to Sunday School, one family enjoys a "continental breakfast" each Sunday morning—consisting of milk, juice, and sweet rolls. Then to help further, they use paper cups and napkins.

It's fun to hear an adult recall the special memories associated with sitting around an old player piano, enjoying the great old-time music.

Singing together as a family can be memory-building fun.

It's a fortunate fellow or girl who, after a date, can bring a partner home to sandwiches or chili or all the yummy things needed for sundaes. Such a tradition makes a much better memory then those gleaned from roaming the streets when it's too dark and too late.

As a schoolgirl I recall coming home to the smell of fresh bread baking and then having a delightful time telling Mother all that happened at school that day while eating warm bread and butter.

I remember,too, breakfasts on holidays when Daddy would

prepare and cook pancakes in special shapes and fry bacon and eggs for us.

Mother taught us to write thank-you notes for gifts or whenever special kindnesses were extended to us. I remember moaning about having to do so, but now I see the value in it, and I'm teaching our children to do so!

At birthday time we were always "king" or "queen" for the day and were privileged to select our very favorite dishes for dinner.

Along with this, tiny children love to have a special birthday cake, perhaps shaped like a merry-go-round, or a choo-choo train frosted to fit specifications, or a cake shaped like a dog, butterfly, or some other animal. This is even more fun if the children are allowed to help with the baking and decorating. The light in our two-year-old Roger's eyes as he told his grandfather, "Me made a doggie happy to you cake," made the horrible mess of coconut and icing in the kitchen so worthwhile.

A yearly visit to the photographer and making family movies and tape recordings are traditions which have lasting value.

Another special activity which is becoming a tradition in our family is to spend an evening looking through baby books, family albums, and viewing our moving pictures. The children are delighted to see what they looked like as babies, and fond memories are impressed upon their minds as pictures recall the highlights of their young lives. I feel confident that as they grow older these pictures will serve to remind them of what in life is most precious and important and will help them to appreciate the past and consequently live the present to the best of their abilities so that the past may always be worth appreciating.

Along with the baby books and albums, we show them our

wedding book containing between its white covers the newspaper announcements of our engagement and marriage, the
names of guests who attended our wedding ceremony, pictures
taken at our reception, the names of the wonderful friends
who came to extend their best wishes on that special night,
the pictures we took on our honeymoon and snapshots of our
first home. We feel that through the pages of that book we
can help prepare our children for the greatest step of their
lives, that of marrying the right person, at the right time, in
the right place.

A part of every child's memory should be some times
spent entirely alone with either Mother or Daddy. Perhaps this
could be while younger children are napping or being privileged
to remain up a few minutes after bedtime for special
companionship. Or maybe this time together could be during a
shopping tour with Mother or while Mother is ironing, or
Mother and child could visit while doing the dishes. I recall as
a teenager that Mother frequently had me set her hair. This
provided a splendid opportunity for me to confide in her and
thereby gain by her interest and advice during those significant
years.

A tradition of character-building value is to encourage your
children each evening as they prepare for bed to tell you one
thing they did during the day which they should improve
upon, and then have them relate the choicest happening of the
day. By the way, such a plan of evaluating the day can be of
merit to parents, too!

At holiday time we have had great fun decorating and
filling cookie buckets (the buckets are white cartons which
painters use to mix paint in and which we decorate with
cheery cuttings from Christmas cards), and giving them to
family members and friends. Also, we've made Valentine
cookies, Easter bunnies, and Halloween cupcakes for little

playmates and cousins. Our children talk about these projects for weeks afterwards and through them learn the joy of giving as well as receiving on such occasions.

The traditions which accompany Thanksgiving are the most typical of our nation. An old-fashioned turkey dinner complete with everything including the pumpkin pie, and all the family present, from Grandmother to the tiniest newcomer, should be an annual event in everyone's life.

The innumerable traditions associated with Christmas are dear to our hearts. One family enacts the Story of the Nativity each Christmas Eve. The family is large and the children anticipate from year to year which part they can portray. Always among the grandchildren is a wee baby who can be the little Christ Child. This has become such a part of their lives that during the entire year each person looks for new ideas, props, and costumes which can be helpful in portraying this beautiful story.

What fun it is to line up in the hallway according to ages at 6 o'clock on Christmas morning, ready for a grand entrance into the living room.

A wise parent will make it a practice to be present whenever a child is performing on a program.

A worthy tradition is for a family to read together for five or ten minutes each morning. It's surprising how many books can be read and how much knowledge can be gained in this manner.

It's been said that parents can give their children a liberal education at the dinner table if they put forth the effort to discuss uplifting, constructive topics.

There is one tradition which every family should enjoy— that of always having good times together.

And finally, crowning our list of traditions is the most influential one of all—that of family prayer. More good can come from that one act than from anything you do as a family.

These traditions are what make families firm and substantial. They give solid roots in the past and hopes for the future. They are little things by themselves, but put together they spell family life.

Instead of your home being just a "short-order house," it can be a hallowed place where children learn life's great lessons, gain proper values, and build up memories which will enrich their lives and help determine their destinies. As a homemaker, establish traditions in your own family. Don't impose them—they must be spontaneous—but do encourage and preserve them. Perhaps there are traditions from your childhood you would like to have perpetuated in your own family, or maybe you can originate some yourself or adopt ideas from others. As an artist in homemaking, these traditions will add color and depth to the great picture you're painting.

FACET NO. 14

IMPERTURBABILITY

An ideal homemaker exercises patience, under-standing, and imperturbability unless controlled anger and reasonable discipline are justified. She will do her best to take those bad days when everything seems to go wrong in her stride, realizing that we need some valleys in order to appreciate the mountains. She needs a sense of humor. She should not take herself, or house, or her children too seriously.

There will be times, even in the best of homes, when everything seems to go wrong. (It is consoling to note, however, that in the best homes where a wonderful manager reigns, these bad days occur far less frequently and are not nearly so drastic in their extent!)

But because there will be times when a half-gallon bottle of milk might be dropped right in the middle of the living room rug, splattering all over the furniture from wall to wall; or when Johnny swings on the floor lamp, causing it to crash to the floor, bringing all the mantle pieces with it; or when Susie spills a bowl of sugar throughout the cupboard; or when the neighborhood children invade the house for drinks of water, leaving a trail of muddy footprints across a freshly waxed floor; what should an ideal homemaker do? We know what she feels like doing, but what is really the best way for her to react? How should a homemaker cope with accidents and upsetting problems?

In an article by Sterling W. Sill he writes: "There is a nice big word which expresses this ability better than any other I know of. It is IMPERTURBABILITY."

He continues by saying: "The dictionary says that to be imperturbable is to be 'incapable of being agitated.' It means to remain calm and controlled, especially in an emergency or under the pressure of serious disturbances or disappointments. A great doctor once said, 'No quality takes an equal rank with imperturbability.'

"The opinion has sometimes been expressed that it may be a good thing to 'let off steam' once in a while or to 'blow one's top.' One can't do this many times before he starts blowing his blood vessels and his nervous system and the success of the organization for which he is responsible. The ancient law still applies that 'whom the gods destroy they first make mad.'

". . . we must learn to deal with these situations without being thrown too far off our course. We need a certain quality of robustness of spirit to enable us to deal fairly and imperturbably with irritations. It is pretty difficult to be thin skinned and great souled at the same time."

Cleon Skousen summed it up well when he said, "A mother should be a perfect imperfectionist." She must train herself to make the best of every situation, she must learn to adjust and take things in her stride, and learn to realize and be prepared for the fact that there will be occasional times when things won't go smoothly.

But remember, if you are on schedule and have things under control BEFORE an emergency arises, you'll be much better prepared to cope with the problem than if you're already upset and behind in your work!

A mother who was nervous about a party she was giving that evening was taking it out on her children. During the course of the hectic day the doorbell rang and she was startled to find her little son on the porch. He told her, "I hoped if I rang the doorbell I could see your company smile. I want to see it so much."

Harold B. Lee said, "There is so much harshness in the world. Don't let your children hear any of it from you. It is all right to turn them on end for a spanking now and then, but don't be harsh with them."

One of the greatest of all virtues is a sense of humor. Certainly a mother needs one! She must not take herself, her house, or her children *too* seriously. Be able to laugh at yourself.

A Mother's Motto could be: "EVERY WORD I SPEAK WILL ADD TO THE PEACE AND HAPPINESS OF MY HOME."

FACET NO. 15

ON HUSBANDS — ALL I ASK

*An ideal homemaker is the type of companion
and wife who merits the appreciation and
cooperation of her husband and helps him to
want to do his part well as a husband, father,
and provider.*

We've talked a great deal about the ideal homemaker. Now
let's discuss the part the husband plays in making a happy
home. In doing so, we're going to consider three questions:
First, should a husband be required to help his wife with the
housework? If so, what should he do and when should he do
it? Second, how can a husband help by not ADDING to his
wife's work? Third, what are a husband's responsibilities around
the home and the yard?

To begin with, it all depends upon your point of view.
The mother of a just-married daughter was asked how her
daughter was getting along. She replied: "Oh, just grand! Why,
she has the most wonderful husband. He helps her with the
dishes and the washing, and does the shopping for her." Then
the mother was asked how her son was who had recently
married. She said: "He has a difficult time. He has the laziest
wife. Why, he has to help her with the dishes and the
washing, and he even has to do the shopping for her."

However, an ambitious, hard-working husband who is doing
his part well to provide for his family shouldn't have to come
home after a hard day's work and help his wife with her
work. Exceptions are times of illness or emergencies, or when
the wife is also working outside the home, or when several
tiny children are in need of attention at the same time. In
these instances, however, his help is invaluable, and a wise wife

will express her appreciation accordingly and not make unreasonable demands.

There are several degrees of helping, however. A lady says her husband is very sweet about helping if she first asks him and then directs his every move. It's fine that he is pleasant and cooperative about helping her, but if he would develop a little spontaneity and ingenuity, his efforts would be of far greater value.

Other husbands help by having their wives run errands for them all the time they're working. "Bring me the screwdriver." "Hand me the hammer." If the husband is high on a ladder or for some reason really needs a little assistance, his wife is glad to work with him. But he should guard against having her take time from her responsibilities to do things which he could do himself.

A husband can help most by following through on a task he performs. For instance, when he does the dishes how wonderful it would be if he would complete the job by cleaning the pots and pans, by rinsing the sink and removing the food particles caught in the drain, and then by sweeping the floor. Or when he undresses the children, what a treat it would be if he would also help them to put away their clothes and shoes.

When the family is preparing for an outing, it is a choice husband who, instead of waiting impatiently in the car, will assist his wife in dressing the children in snowsuits and boots or in helping with some of the other last-minute chores which must be done before leaving the house.

A wife, if she is reasonable, doesn't expect a great deal of help from her husband, but she does want GOOD help. Ten minutes a day of the right type of help—on a volunteer basis, coupled with the ability to follow through until a task is completed, and combined with a willing attitude—could make a world of difference to her.

II

A husband should not ADD to his wife's work. He can avoid making more work for her through his thoughtfulness and consideration. A thoughtful husband can save his wife from both worrying and waiting if he will call her if he is going to be detained.

He should put away his own personal belongings such as clothes, shoes, books, and papers. Some husbands leave a trail of hat, coat, briefcase, and papers clear through the house as they arrive home, and a similar trail each morning of slippers, bathrobe, towel, and shaving supplies as they leave for work. A thoughtful husband should also clean up any mess he might make in doing repair jobs or creative work. He should avoid tracking in dirt and grass from the yard, and he should wash dirty hands before touching the furniture and woodwork. Not only does this aid the wife greatly, but it sets an excellent example for the children!

One evening after doing the chores on the farm, several grown boys, along with their father, came in the house, took some oranges from the kitchen and sat down around the fireplace and began to peel and eat the oranges. Then they all left, leaving orange juice and peelings scattered over the rug. Shortly the busy wife and mother had to gather up all the peelings, throw them away, and take care of the juice spots as best she could. How easy it would have been for each man to have taken a plate and paper napkins with him, thereby saving the homemaker the effort of this additional task.

Some husbands have been well trained before marriage to be neat and tidy about their personal belongings and to be thoughtful and considerate, but others enter marriage with much to learn. Many wives whose husbands are "messer-uppers" just tolerate the situation and become slaves to their husbands, forever cleaning up after them. Other wives nag their husbands to distraction over the matter and only make things worse. (There are two sides to nagging, however, according to this definition: "Nagging is frequent repetition of something that should have been paid attention to and corrected the first time it was mentioned.")

A husband complained to a friend because his wife was always asking for ten dollars. He said, "Why, she's asked me for ten dollars every day this week."

His friend inquired, "What is she doing with all that money?"

"I don't know. I haven't given her anything yet," replied the husband.

The ideal way to solve the problem is for the husband and wife to sit down together when neither is rushed or irritable and intelligently and maturely discuss the situation. Talking things over solves many problems. An essential factor in a happy marriage is to keep the lines of communication open— build a bridge, not a wall. We mentioned under FACET NO. 13 the value of family councils. Its is also an excellent idea for the parents to meet together as the Board of Directors.

Remember, you can tell a person anything and get away with it if you smile at him!

A magic formula is: "I'm sorry. Please forgive me."

So often duty says, "I have done all that is required." Love says, "What more can I do?" Don't go only fifty percent of the way—often it is necessary to go ninety-five percent of the way, or even a hundred percent.

Then if for some reason a good discussion does not do the trick, here are a couple of methods which have been recommended as being highly successful:

The first suggestion is the theory of, "I'll do something for you if you'll do something for me." Perhaps there is something special your husband would like you to bake. (One husband has been asking his wife for forty years to bake bread and she hasn't yet given it a try.) Then in turn he could strive to overcome some fault or do something for you.

Perhaps a list kept in a conspicuous spot of duties your husband should do would help him. Such a list is a better reminder than a wife's nagging, it could help him to plan and organize regarding his obligations around the house, and he could experience the satisfaction of crossing off items as they're completed.

(CAUTION! Use a great deal of discretion before trying any one of the following types of suggestions on your husband. If feelings between you are good, one of these "shockers" might be just what he needs to be an even better husband. However, if there is tension between you or if your husband is extra sensitive, one of these suggestions could be a disastrous spark in setting off an explosion. If your problems are deep, see a marriage counselor.)

One young bride suggests this type of approach: Her husband was in the habit of leaving everything lying around, so after a couple of exasperating days she began to pick up and hide the items she found around the house. Finally when he was about down to nothing to wear he became quite concerned. He asked her what the trouble was and she presented her "collection" to him. (It's a good idea, however, to make such a presentation after dinner when you've served your husband one of his favorite dishes!) This man got the point and has been a model husband ever since.

Another young wife said her husband hung his trousers over the top of doors in the bedroom and bathroom instead of putting them away in his closet, She had talked to him about it several times, but the trousers still draped the doors. Finally one day she gathered several pair up and tossed them very carelessly over a hanger in the closet. Needless to say, he was upset to find his trousers in that condition and told his wife what he thought about the way she had hung them up. She explained to him that she had wrinkled them intentionally and would continue to do so any time trousers were left hanging around. He, too, learned his lesson well and hangs his trousers in the closet now, thereby keeping both his home and his clothes neater.

A friend's husband always threw his coat on the floor in a corner of the back porch when he came home from outside farm chores. One day he was astonished to find three six-penny nails driven in a row in his "coat corner." When asked to explain, his wife said, "For ten years I've been trying to get you to hang up your coat, and I finally decided if you're going to insist upon hanging it on the floor, I'd have to put some nails there for you to hang it on." The coat is hung in the closet now.

One lady reported that a much-needed coat of paint was applied to their living room by her husband when finally in desperation she scribbled over the walls with water colors.

Sometimes a procrastinating husband can be embarrassed or humiliated into action by his wife's giving up in desperation and doing the job herself or by calling in a neighbor to do it. It's better to have it be on his conscience than on her nerves!

One of these appeals should work. If it doesn't you had better learn to live with the problem and accept this as your philosophy: "God grant us the serenity to accept the things we cannot change, the courage to change the things we can, and the wisdom to know the difference."

Always remember that you cannot expect perfection in a mate unless you can also offer it. Don't allow one or two irksome traits in your husband to blot out the dozens of wonderful things which he is. Every rose has its thorn—never let the thorn prevent you from enjoying the beauty of the flower.

III

Now, what are a husband's responsibilities around the home and yard? One Saturday evening at a banquet, Marion D. Hanks commented that he had spent the afternoon around his home "honey-doing." When questioned as to what he meant, he said, "Oh, it was 'honey do this' and 'honey do that.' "

It is a choice husband who will carry out little projects which need attention for the *physical* well-being of the home such as fixing leaking taps, repairing loose door hinges, and mending broken toys. A husband, too, should take pride in his home and yard and do his part to keep things in excellent condition, or else provide the means to hire someone to keep things maintained.

A wife really does need help from her husband in regards to heavy or mechanical work. Help him to feel that he is needed! Help him to want to do his part! Remember, people will do anything if they really want to. The way to make your husband want to do his part well is for you to do your own work as a homemaker so beautifully that he will want to measure up to his own responsibilities in this partnership.

A husband should be ambitious and conscientious and thereby do his utmost to provide for his family's *material* needs. Not only should money be available for their use, but a wise husband and father will allot some of it to them for their needs. One woman said that she was in desperate need of a new pair of shoes, and although money for the shoes was available, her husband just didn't quite get around to giving it to her. Finally, she put a pie shell around the old shoes, baked them, and served them to her husband for dinner along with the speech, "If they're good enough for me, then they're good enough for you."

An ideal husband and father will work with his wife in the *guiding and training of the children* and will be a companion and teacher to them. There is much more to being a father than merely to help create the children and provide for their physical needs! Good parents will present a united front in disciplining their children. Both mother and father should learn the best methods of discipline (outstanding and interesting books on this subject are available at any public library), and be firm and fair in all they do.

A father can do much to help by assuming full responsibility of several of the young children when the family is away from home. For instance, Daddy could take complete charge of one or two children—watching that they stay close, supervising their behavior, and helping them with any eating that is done—while Mother tends to the needs of the tinest children.

A good father is a companion to his children and fills a great need in their lives by expressing love and affection for them and by being interested in them.

"One morning my small son said to me at breakfast, 'Daddy, may I read to you? I got nine out of ten for reading at school yesterday.'

" 'Very good,' said I, hardly glancing from my paper.

" 'May I?'

" 'Eh? May you what?' I demanded—being in haste, and wishful to glance over the news and finish breakfast in next to no time.

" 'May I read to you?'

" 'Well, not now, son! There's no time.'

"So off I went to catch a bus.

"Home that evening, I told my little son that I would listen to his reading as soon as I had had my supper. But somebody called, and I had to see him. And then somebody else called, and I had to engage him. And finally I went into my son's bedroom, and found him fast asleep, his cheeks wet with tears, a school reader open on the bed.

"Thus, through this experience, I learned my lesson—to love him a little more, and myself a little less."

A good husband will also provide *socially* for his wife. First, he will be companionable. "True love and companionship consist not in gazing at one another, but in looking forward together." Evenings with your husband need not be idle times. Instead they should be productive hours when reading, studying, good music, mending, and sewing are enjoyed. You needn't always both be doing the same thing at the same time in order to enjoy companionship. If you have a common goal and if there is a good feeling between you, you can feel a bond of companionship even though you are busy at the sink in the kitchen and he is busy at the typewriter in his den—or even though you are across the city from one another.

Second, it is most commendable and essential to plan and do many things together. The marriage vows shouldn't put an end to your courtship. Continue to go out together, to play together, to visit with each other, and to enjoy each other's presence.

Tertullian said, "Woman was not taken from the head of man, for she was not intended to be his ruler; nor from his feet, for she was not intended to be his slave; but from his side, for she was to be his companion."

A husband can do a great deal for his wife and toward keeping the wheels of matrimony running smoothly by being conscious of her *emotional* needs. An ideal husband will be thoughtful and considerate of his wife. He will express frequent appreciation for what she is doing—just a sentence a day would help her so much! He will speak well of her in public. "The

real heart and soul of a man are measured by the consideration and understanding and respect he shows to women. By a
man's ideal of womanhood we may know the degree of his
manhood." (David Starr Jordan.) He will treat her to surprises
and good times just as he did during their courting days. Little
things like presenting a flower or other gift for an anniversary,
or sending a lovely Valentine means so much and makes for
harmony and happiness in the home.

An old Scotsman was standing by the graveside of his wife.
A friend near him commented, "You certainly had a wonderful
wife, aye, Mike?"

Mike slowly replied, "Aye, and I nearly told her so once."

We as wives and mothers need to know that we are
appreciated. A fine husband and father I know not only
expresses frequent appreciation to his wife for all she does, but
he even helps the children to realize what their mother means
to them. For instance, one evening he took them to their
clothes closet and pointed out their clean, pressed clothing.
The father further called their attention to many of the other
tasks which the mother had performed to make things
comfortable and lovely for them.

Special thoughtful gestures, beyond those things which are
expected, on the part of the husband give the homemaker a
personal uplift and help to strengthen the bonds of love and
companionship. It's refreshing if a husband will occasionally
offer to baby-sit so the mother can enroll in an adult
education class or engage in some other worthwhile activity.
What fun for both husband and wife if he will suggest from
time to time that he make pizza or sundaes—while she relaxes
after the children are in bed, or gets right up from the table
and does the dishes without any bidding—simply because he
loves her and wants to help.

An ideal husband will provide *spiritual* leadership as the

head of the family. Although a husband and wife have equal responsibility in making a home and in rearing a family, they have different responsibilities. After a discussion has been held, it should be the father who voices the decision which has been reached. Even though it is the mother who plans the time for family councils and family prayers, it should be the father who calls the family together and presides at these occasions. An old proverb says, "It is a sad house where the hen crows louder than the rooster."

A person tends to become what you think of him. Think and speak highly of your husband and he will grow to fit the part if he doesn't already. Praise him for the fine things he is, be openly appreciative and grateful to him for what he does. You will find that he will respond by repeating his good deeds and by doing other things to please you.

It is a good idea to make a list (and refer to it frequently) of all your husband's good points and the many things he does for the well-being of you and your family. Capitalize on his virtues rather than his shortcomings. Think back to the qualities which first attracted you to him. Always keep in sight the things which caused you to fall in love—and this will help you to stay in love!

The Bible tells us that neither the man nor the woman is complete without the other. We do need one another, and together we can be much finer people than when we are alone. Certainly it is true that a wife, through the proper approach, can do much to help her husband help her, and also to succeed in his own personal life.

A woman can do a great deal to send her husband either up or down the ladder of success. A Texan was asked one time what part his wife played in his becoming a millionaire. He replied, "Oh, she had everything to do with it." Then he was asked what he was before he married. "I was a multi-millionaire."

Every man needs a good wife—one who will love and support him. It once was said, "Long live King George the Fifth." Another person added, "Yes, and long live Queen Mary, the four-fifths."

Here's a poem, dedicated to our husbands:

When a man asks a maid
   And she says she'll be his
It's the man's fondest hope
   She'll stay just as she is;
But the maid, ere she's married,
   Has drafted a plan
For complete alterations
   To make on her man.
A maid, to a man, is a vision ethereal—
A man, to a maid, is a piece of material.

                           Burge Buzzele

FACET NO. 16

BUDGETING — NOT SUCH A BAD WORD

An ideal homemaker is skilled in the handling of money, in planned shopping, in careful storage, and in clever preparation of food. She is able to conserve the family's possessions through good management. She does not economize and follow a budget out of self-pity, but because it is a challenge to get the very most out of the resources available.

The bride, white of hair, is stooped over her cane,
Her footsteps, uncertain, need guiding.
While down the church aisle, with a wan toothless smile,
The groom in a wheelchair comes riding.
And who is this elderly couple, thus wed?
You'll find when you've closely explored it,
That here is that rare, most conservative pair
Who waited until they could afford it.

Author Unknown

That's a change from the countless young couples today who have succumbed to the easy credit plans and who are paying for everything in their homes and all at the same time!

It has been wisely stated that no man is rich who spends more than he earns, and no man is poor who earns more then he spends. In the next few pages are some budget ideas which will help you to spend within your income and thereby not only be "rich" but also enjoy the peace of mind and sense of security which comes through properly managed finances.

We've already discussed that in order to get the most out of one's time, the minutes of the day must be planned and budgeted. Certainly the same technique holds true in getting the most out of our nickles, dimes, and dollars.

Just as some people never have enough time, so do many people frequently have too much month left over at the end of their money. The solution to this problem lies in planning—or budgeting.

The first step toward good financial management is to secure a book in which a record of income and expenses can be kept. A business has to keep books in order to operate, and because marriage is a partnership—it can even become a corporation—books must be kept in order for it to operate successfully.

A record book can be purchased for a nominal cost in dime stores—or some banks and insurance companies present complimentary budget books. Most budget books contain in-structions for using them effectively.

In general, the book will suggest that you begin by determining your NET BUDGETABLE INCOME or "take-home pay." This net budgetable income is derived by substracting from your gross income such amounts as withholding taxes, group insurance, and any other payroll deductions.

Second, distribute your net budgetable income into cate-gories such as food, housing and transportation, clothing, pledged contributions, church donations, installment payments, emergency fund, life insurance and savings, education and recreation, and miscellaneous (children's allowances, Christmas fund, vacation money, and other extras).

A rule of thumb is that, based on an average income, you should spend approximately thirty percent of your net budget-able income for food; twenty-eight percent for housing and transportation (this does not include car payments); and ten percent for clothing. Your emergency fund should equal the amount of two or more months' take-home pay. Life insurance and savings should be based upon one's obligations toward his family and society. Here again, a rule of thumb is that your life insurance should equal three times your annual income, at least.

Installment payments should not exceed thirteen percent of your net budgetable income. Some families spend as high as twenty percent of their money towards installment programs—but if you find yourself in this position you're sitting on thin ice and you had better take a closer look at your spending habits. Certainly the lower your installment buying is, the better off you are. Purchases made with cash do away with the added cost of carrying charges or interest, and this way you are never "payment pinched" and you don't run the risk of having an item repossessed. With the exception of large investments, such as a home, it is a worthy goal for every family to learn to save and then pay cash for the things they buy.

For personal growth and development, it is important to allocate at least five percent of your budgetable income towards education and recreation. The amount of money you spend for pledged contributions is strictly a personal matter. The remainder of your money can go towards miscellaneous items and a sound, long-range savings or investment program. Don't be too alarmed if this margin is slim during the early years of marriage; one must build a foundation before he can put the roof on!

These ideas are only a guide to good spending. Everyone's budget has to be worked out on an individual basis. The main thing is to know, instead of wonder, where your money is going, to manage your income wisely—to spend less than you earn—and you'll sleep well at night and be rich!

After allocating your money, the first step is to spend it wisely. Let's first consider marketing. Your greatest savings here

comes from shopping from a list (and sticking to the list!) and planning menus a week in advance. (See FACET NO. 7.) Learn to shop by following the Thursday newspaper ads, and whenever possible buy foods, particularly meat and produce, which are in season and consequently are more economical. Food items purchased in quantity (such as case goods, staple products in bulk, and the largest jars and boxes on the shelves) further help to s-t-r-e-t-c-h your food dollar. Powdered milk (for cooking and baking purposes and to extend whole milk); a butter substitue; small brown eggs (they're just like large, white ones once they are cracked); cooked cereal in place of the prepared packaged variety; and flour, baking powder, and other ingredients (plus a good recipe and a little ambition) rather than bakery products will stretch that dollar even farther.

The second step, after planned shopping, is careful storage of food. Be certain to place items where they will be least affected by moisture, light, and temperature changes. And by all means rotate items in your cupboards so that nothing is kept unused in the rear so long that it spoils.

Third, excel in clever preparation of food. This is where it is fun to be thrifty! And here is where a most significant savings come in—an old Scottish proverb reminds us: "A woman can throw out more with a teaspoon than a man can bring home with a wheelbarrow."

You'll save money if you cook in quantity and freeze part of it for future use. (We discussed this under FACET NO. 5 because it saves time, too!)

With a little imagination, the use of left-overs can give you two meals for the price of one. One ingenious cook freezes her left-overs in small foil pie plates or custard cups. Then when she has a good supply, she warms them in the oven and has a smorgasbord that evening.

You can make your own TV dinners from leftovers.

Spread leftover mashed potatoes out in a thin layer on a buttered baking sheet, dot with butter, and slide under the broiler until golden brown. Cut in squares and remove with a pancake turner. Serve piping hot.

Wrap leftover pieces of fried chicken in aluminum foil before storing them in the refrigerator; pop them into the oven, still wrapped, to reheat when you plan to serve them again. Stored in this manner they will retain their freshly fried savor for several days.

Soups, stews, chili, macaroni, spaghetti, and rice casseroles are good economy dishes. However, when a meal is obviously budget fare, a clever cook will offset it a little by preparing hot biscuits, a special salad, or the family's favorite dessert.

The cost of baby food can be cut down by making your own in an Osterizer or blender. The food can then be frozen in individual ice cubes—a cube is just the right size for a serving.

Food, attractively prepared and served, will help to disguise attempts on the part of the cook to economize. Arrange it in an appealing manner on the plate and brighten it up a bit with some parsley, paprika, or other type of garnish. Oatmeal, served with raisin faces, helps youngsters to find it tempting. One mother reports that she was having difficulty getting her family to eat apple sauce until she colored it pink.

The names, or titles, of dishes have a definite psychological effect. Mrs. Vance Hyde, an outstanding budget cook and writer on the subject says: "... a sense of drama in titling your creations will make all the difference in how they are accepted. We never have stew or hash at our house. Or rather, we never have a dish called stew or hash. But Mystery Casserole and Persian Blend are real favorites. They (the family) consider they're eating like royalty when I serve Crown

Roast of Frankfurters, too, which is probably the cheapest company meal in the world. I string hot dogs on a length of heavy string through the middle and again at one end, tie the strings so that the franks will stand on end like a crown roast. The girls (Mrs. Hyde's daughters) then fill the middle with seasoned mashed potatoes and we pop it in the oven to heat through. . . ."

You can take the monotony out of meatloaf with a similar variation. Bake the meat loaf in a well-greased ring mold or angel food cake pan. When you are ready to serve it, unmold it on a large plate, fill the center with creamed or buttered vegetables and call it Vegetable Meat Ring.

Food tastes better if it looks attractive. Even economical dinners can look special.

Homemade products, instead of the commercial type, are good budget boosters. For instance, home-made bread can be a source of savings to a family, and once you as a homemaker get it down to a system, you can mix up a batch of bread in less than fifteen minutes. Besides being a money saver, your family will love it. One woman mentioned that she never has to worry about her husband looking at another woman so long as she bakes bread. A pair of darling little twins who are just learning to talk call anything in the bread family "toast." Recently their mother put some homemade bread on the table and they said, "mmmmmmmmmmm, cake!"

Home-styled haircuts can save a family with little boys considerable money. Clipper sets with plastic gauges to insure an even cut are available on the market.

Home-sewn clothing often saves enough money to give you two or more articles for the price of one. Teenage girls, particularly, should be encouraged to sew for themselves. A wise mother will either teach them to sew herself or arrange for them to enroll in a sewing course. Sewing does more than just save money. It teaches a girl to be creative and rewards her with satisfaction and the pride of accomplishment.

Shopping sales can be advantageous IF you are a good judge of quality and IF you have enough sales resistance not to buy something you don't need even if it is a bargain.

As a good homemaker, you'll not only manage money well yourself, but you will guide your children in household economics. A three-year-old can form the habit of turning a light off each time he leaves a room; older children can work with you and thereby learn as you plan and shop. In fact, children should be given an allowance for the prime purpose of learning how to handle money. They should even gradually assume partial responsibility for the family's finances and do some marketing for food and shopping for clothing themselves. A dollar mistake now might save them a thousand dollar unwise expenditure later on! We gave two of our little girls, ages four and five, a dollar bill and let them go to a toy department to buy a birthday present for a younger sister. A little later I went to get them and found that instead of the dollar, they had a handful of dimes. I asked them what happened to the dollar. The five-year-old answered: "We went to the check stand and had the dollar changed into dimes. We can think better in dimes."

A good homemaker will further guide the family in being economy-conscious by teaching them to properly care for what they already have. This means putting toys where they belong (FACET NO. 12) and treating clothing and furnishings with respect. It's sad if the family income must be spent on replacing things. Take care of what you have and then the money can go for items which will help you to progress and improve your standard of living.

And even more important than giving your children tricks and ideas is to instill within them, through your attitude, example, and training, the conviction that it is smart to economize and that it can be fun to be thrifty. Extravagance and waste are sinful, regardless of how much money is available. Even if you do have ample income for your needs, handling it well could afford you the means to help some deserving person who isn't as fortunate as you, or it could provide for you a rich, lasting experience such as a trip abroad.

As a homemaker, specialize in sensible money spending. You'll never be accused of throwing out more with a teaspoon than your husband can bring home with a wheelbarrow. Instead, by making the most of your money (not necessarily by making the most money) you'll spend less than you earn and be rich!

FACET NO. 17

THAT SPECIAL SOMETHING

And after all of these facets have made our ideal homemaker like a sparkling diamond, she will add a few other special facets of her own to set her apart from all the rest.

There is something very special about you. You have gifts and talents which are your very own. Discover them, if you haven't already, and develop them.

Perhaps you are gifted with a sense of humor and are a source of fun and delight to all who know you. Maybe yours is the quality of making friends, of helping people to feel happy and at ease wherever you go. Are you an especially thoughtful person—one who is always extending a kind gesture to gladden another's heart?

Do you have that certain touch in arranging flowers beautifully or in wrapping a gift in a particularly attractive way?

Perhaps you dance or sing or play, and thereby make this world a brighter place through a graceful, rhythmic dance, a beautiful song, or a soul-thrilling musical rendition.

Maybe you are creative and can paint a picture or write a poem. Or can you design and sew a dress or bake a pie or a cake? Can you produce something which is a testimony to your ability, your energy, your imagination—YOU?

You have a special talent, probably more than one. Develop them for the benefit and service of mankind. Develop them so that in your brilliant diamond, some facets will shine a bit brighter and give you that special something.

FACET NO. 18

JUST FOR TODAY

In summary, an ideal homemaker is an artist in general management so that her home is able to function at its peak performance and fulfill its lofty purpose and so that she along with her husband and children can reflect the joy, order, and progressive spirit therin. She does not try to accomplish this thirty years at a time, but strives to practice being an artist in management and homemaking JUST FOR TODAY.

Perfection is a process, not an event. Don't be discouraged if you are not able to reach your goal overnight. Practice makes perfect—just so it is the right kind of practice.

A woman can't be expected to be a qualified nurse or secretary without adequate training and some experience. Neither can she be a good homemaker without the proper training and experience.

With experience comes a kind of Sixth Sense which tells you just how much is a pinch of salt; it informs you, without unnecessary peeks, when a cake is ready to come out of the oven; it gives you a nudge to investigate when Junior has been a little too quiet for too long.

Someone once said, "Life by the yard is hard; inch by inch it's a cinch." Strive to master these facets one at a time. Put a good idea into practice JUST FOR TODAY, and finally many days of trying that hard (you can do anything if you truly WANT to) will lead you to the glorious goal of being an artist in home management and a worthy wife and mother.

Ralph Waldo Emerson said, "That which we persist in doing becomes easier for us to do; not that the nature of the thing itself is changed, but that our power to do is increased."

FACET NO. 19

THE POWER OF PRAYER

An ideal homemaker will seek divine guidance through prayer, so that her home may be an extension of heaven and so that she may walk in partnership with God in rearing the precious little souls he has sent her.

An ancient Chinese proverb reads: "The man is head of the house, but the woman is the heart of the home." It is true that you as a homemaker set the spiritual temperature of your home. Your feelings and responses are reflected in the atmosphere about you.

Prayer can be the passport to the spiritual power you need to help you be an ideal homemaker and to help you be worthy of the trust that is yours in raising children. Prayer can lift you up when you are discouraged; you can fulfill your responsibilities more effectively if you pray about them; through prayer you can set the noblest of all examples for your children.

The book of Proverbs (31:27) in the Bible says, "She looketh well to the ways of her household. . . ."

An old English proverb tells us: "Prayer should be the key to the day and the lock of the night." As a homemaker, make this part of your life and you will find your activities meaningful and your strength and abilities equal to your tasks.

Surely if you seek his help, the Lord will bless you in looking well to the ways of your household and in making your home a house of God or an extension of heaven here on earth.

FACET NO. 20

HAVE A GLORY

And finally, an ideal homemaker, through having these many facets in her brilliant diamond, will be able to take pride in her noble calling and in the great work she is doing.

As a young boy, Mark Twain took a steamboat trip down the Mississippi River. He was a typically curious lad and explored the ship from bow to stern. His wanderings led to the engine room. He recalled many years later that he had never seen a dirtier place in his life. Slimy oil and bilge water covered the deck around the bottom of the engine. Dirty, greasy rags were strewn about the floor. Grease that had been collecting for years covered the engine. The sight of that room was unforgettably repulsive to Mark Twain.

Years late he happened to be on the same boat again and retraced the steps he had taken as a boy. Once again he visited the engine room.

This time an incredible contrast met his eyes. Gone from the deck were all the oil and bilge water. The filthy rags had disappeared. All of the grease had been wiped from the engine; the brass and copper parts had been polished until they gleamed!

Sitting next to the engine was a jolly, plump, colored man, wearing on his moon-shaped face one of the most pleasant expressions Mark Twain had ever beheld.

Mr. Twain commended the engineman on the tremendous improvement that had taken place and asked how such a startling contrast could be accounted for. The old engineman replied, "Mr. Twain, I've got a Glory."

His glory, he said, was having the finest engine room on the Mississippi River. Without doubt, he had succeeded.

There's a vital lesson here. Each of us needs a glory in our homemaking.

* * *

May you truly be successful and happy in the greatest of all careers, and may someone someday write about you as was written of "Grandmother"—listing the numerous worthwhile accomplishments of your day and then recording that at nightfall you were able to play "When You Come to the End of a Perfect Day."

This will surely be so, because as John Ruskin said, "When love and skill work together, expect a masterpiece."

INDEX

NOTES

NOTES